An Unofficial & Unsanctioned

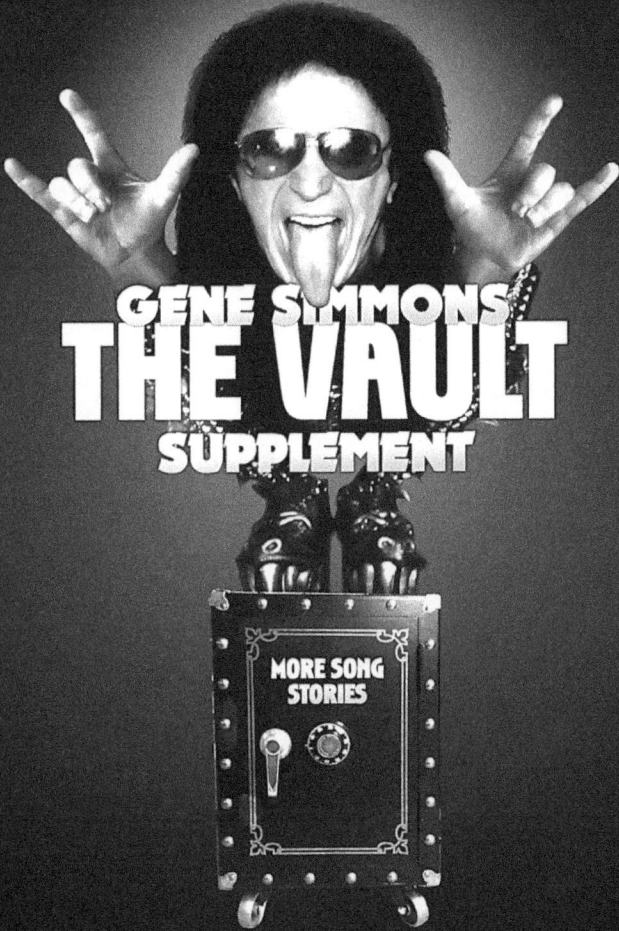

GENE SIMMONS
THE VAULT
SUPPLEMENT

MORE SONG
STORIES

JULIAN GILL

sup·ple·ment

noun
/ˈsəpləmənt/ ◀))

1. something that completes or enhances something else when added to it.
   "the handout is a **supplement to** the official manual"
   synonyms: addition, accessory, supplementation, supplementary, extra, add-on, adjunct, appendage; More

Revision: 06/25/2023 06:23:56 AM

ISBN-13: 978-0-9997765-1-3

Contents

GENE SIMMONS

A special note for those of you who are listening to the soundtrack music in the background. You may not recognize some of the music on here, because it has never been released. These are demo versions of songs that will be appearing next year in my GENE SIMMONS 100 BOXSET – 100 songs that have never been released. Enjoy.

"Weapons"
"Carnival Of Souls"
"Sweet And Dirty Love"
"Am I Losing My Mind"
"Damn I'm Good"
"Every Day Above Ground"
"Everybody Knows"
"Granny Takes A Trip"
"I Turn To Stone"
"It 2"
"Jellyroll"
"You Kill Me"
"Rock It Hard"
"Mirage"
"Radio Active"
"Rotten II"
"Rotten To The Core"
"Son Of 7th"
"Too Hot Too Cold"
"Weapons Of Mass Destruction"
"You're My Reason For Living"
"I Wanna Rule The World"
"Into The Void"
"I Am Yours"
"Rain Keeps Falling"
"Take It Like A Man"

All songs written by Gene Simmons except "Carnival Of Souls" (Simmons, Van Zen). Publishing: Gene Simmons Worldwide ASCAP.

SANCTUARY 06074-88392-9

SPEAKING IN TONGUES

The "Vault" was a long time coming. Many of the songs included were teased in the "Speaking in Tongues" DVD released in September 2004!

About The Vault

Gene had been planning a box set of his unreleased material for more than 15 years by the time his vision was realized. Under various titles such as "Monster," "Alter Ego," or simply "100," there were more than enough suggestions about what Gene's goals were, and in some cases what the contents would include. Unfortunately, various ideas never came to fruition, primarily due to Gene's issues with the modern distribution model as the remnants of the music business moved further and further away from the traditional methods he understood best. Approaching various labels, Gene simply wasn't interested in releasing 150–200 songs in a manner that they would immediately appear on file-sharing platforms — the memories of Napster had clearly not dimmed with the passage of time.

For Gene the question was about how his perception of the industry: "The record industry is in such a mess. I called for what it was when college kids first started download music for free — that they were crooks. I told every record label I spoke with that they just lit the fuse to their own bomb that was going to explode from under them and put them on the street... How are you going to deliver it? How are you going to get paid for it if people can just get it for free? ... The record industry doesn't have a f*cking clue how to make money. It's only their fault for letting foxes get into the henhouse and then wondering why there's no eggs or chickens. Every little college kid, every freshly scrubbed little kid's face should have been sued off the face of the earth. They should have taken their houses and cars and nipped it right there in the beginning. Those kids are putting 100,000 to a million people out of work. How can you pick on them? They've got freckles. That's a crook. He may as well be wearing a bandit's mask" (Billboard, 11/12/2007).

As early as 2003 Gene was teasing archival material. For his "Sex Money KISS" audio book release on CD, he included a bonus CD featuring "Everybody Knows" and "You're My Reason for Living." The following year, when Gene released his "Speaking in Tongues" speaking-tour DVD via Sanctuary Records, it seemed the release of a "Gene Simmons 100 Box set" was imminent. Numerous demo samples were featured on that release, many of which would ultimately be included on "The Vault." Nothing materialized... In 2007, as part of the season 1 DVD release of the Gene Simmons Family Jewels, Gene included a sampler CD featuring "Rain Keeps Fallin'" and "You're My Reason for Living." The "Monster" box set was expected to appear in 2008, along with a second KISS archival collection. In 2010 Gene tweeted that he was working every day, on and off, on a release of perhaps as many as 200 tunes. Neither it nor any KISS archival release materialized, and the title was ultimately used by KISS for their 2012 studio album.

By 2009, Gene was referring to the box as "Alter Ego," liking the superhero parallel that the title suggested. However, Gene felt that not all people might understand the phrase. Eventually, Rhino, a label that had successfully carved out a niche featuring high-quality archival releases, were willing to do the project Gene's way, and keep it out of stores. For Gene, selling less units at a higher per unit price made more business sense, as did cutting out the middleman. But he also wanted to have a personal relationship with the fans during the transaction. He hoped that those paying a premium for the experience would be less willing to illegally distribute the material or share it with friends. One packaging idea, a silver Halliburton briefcase, was simply too expensive to reproduce. With Rhino, Gene simply sketched out an idea of a rolling vault on wheels. And during one late night conversation following the death of Prince, Keith Valcourt suggested the name "Vault." The physical size of the "Vault," in some ways, was as far as one could get from the ethereal digital release. It was a big, brash, and heavy rejection of digital (though ironically leveraged the digital domain for the download of a free track for purchasers of the set).

(Gene during the Los Angeles "Songs & Stories" session)

This **unofficial** & **unsanctioned** Gene Simmons "Vault" Supplement is an attempt to add additional context, clarity and information to the song notes included in the exquisite "Vault" book. It doesn't claim to attempt to be a replacement for that work!

(Lonely Vaults, waiting patiently for their forever homes!)

— Key —

✪   Song previously released, albeit in a similar, non-identical form.

⊙   Song previously released by another artist.

✶   Song re-released elsewhere after the "Vault."

Disk 01

Running time: 54:28

01. Are You Ready

(3:09) - Gene Simmons
Recorded: 2007/8
Source:
Studio:

Specifically chosen to start the Vault, this anthemic cast off was recorded with Tommy Thayer and Eric Singer. While Gene has suggested that it was omitted from a KISS album in favor of the likes of songs like "Psycho Circus" and "I Pledge Allegiance to the State of Rock and Roll," it more likely dates from the "Sonic Boom" / "Monster" era. It was mentioned at that time for possible inclusion on the latter album; as a rewrite of an earlier song with the same title. Initially, the song was used as the primary sample used to promote the Vault and was available as a digital download as part of purchaser's Vault pre-packs. This song was first performed live by the Gene Simmons Band on Feb. 16, 2018 at the Lynn Auditorium in Lynn, MA. During the song's intro, Gene suggested that it had been written in 1999.

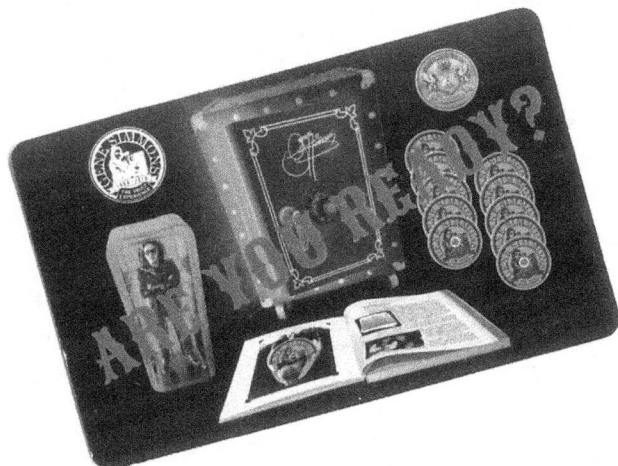

(The pre-pack download card providing purchasers with their first listen to a full song from the "Vault.")

02. I Turn to Stone

(4:14) – Gene Simmons
Recorded: Feb 1993
Source:
Studio:

This track was among the dozens of ideas and songs submitted by Gene for the "Psycho Circus" album. With similarities to "Domino," Gene initially recorded the intro to the song on a tape-recorder in a hotel room before cutting a more fleshed-out version with Tommy Thayer. A sample of this song was previously teased on Gene's "Speaking in Tongues" DVD in 2004.

03. Juliet

(2:52) - Gene Simmons / Ken Tamplin
Recorded: 1993/4
Source:
Studio: Ken Tamplin Studio

Included in the Vault's preview sonic montage, this Ken Tamplin co-write dates from the "Revenge" era. Ken plays guitars on the recording which is musically backed by a drum machine. The song features a strong Living Colour "Cult of Personality"-like riff. According to Gene, the title is a play on Joliet, which is just down Rte. 7 from Romeoville in Illinois.

04. Hey You

(3:44) - Gene Simmons / Ken Tamplin
Recorded: 1993/4
Source:
Studio: Ken Tamplin Studio

Included in the Vault's preview sonic montage, this powerful call-out track was recorded at Ken's home studio. The recording features prominent bass work by Simmons.

05. I Confess

(3:40) - Gene Simmons / Ken Tamplin
Recorded: 1993/4
Source:

Studio: Ken Tamplin Studio

The third of the Tamplin songs, this is a demo of the title released on KISS' "Carnival of Souls" in 1997. Naturally, as is often the case with a demo, many of the musical elements were changed when properly recorded though the guitar work provides a fascinating contrast to that on the finished version. This demo was likely recorded during the summer of 1994.

06. Legends Never Die ⊙

(4:23) - Gene Simmons / Adam Mitchell / Micki Free
Recorded: 1982
Source:
Studio: Record Plant Studios, Los Angeles, CA

A semi-biographical song about a person Gene had known during school who had always wanted to be in a band but had eventually taken his own life. KISS recorded this song during the "Creatures of the Night" sessions. However, the song was purportedly not included because Paul was not overly fond of it. Gene later simply took the KISS track and added Wendy O. Williams' vocals to it for her "WOW" album and as a result Eric Carr received a drumming credit. Micki was credited on acoustic guitar. Musically, down to the solo, this song is the same. The song was originally titled "When the Legend Dies" and credited to Micki Free and Gene Simmons. In 2002 Doro, who had previously covered "Only You" and recorded Simmons' penned songs, recorded a cover of the song. A sample of this song was included in the Vault's preview sonic montage.

07. Something Wicked This Way Comes ⊙

(3:48) - Gene Simmons
Recorded: 1988
Source:
Studio: Artisan Sound Recorders, Studio C

While Doro later recorded this song for her 1990 album (which was produced by Gene), the song had originally been under consideration for KISS' use on the "Hot in the Shade" album the previous year. It was later cut from the album but was included in track-listings distributed in PR material. With Gene's later writing, both on "Carnival of Souls" and the general theme of "Psycho Circus," the song shares a title with Ray Bradbury's Gothic novel which is about a diabolical carnival — led by mysterious ringmaster Mr. Dark — that visits a small Illinois town. Recorded with Bruce Kulick on lead guitar, this version of the track cuts much of the unnecessary repetition of the primary riff that features on the circulating demo. It was likely recorded with Mikey Davis engineering.

(Once in the author's collection...)

08. Hand of Fate

(3:12) - Gene Simmons
Recorded: 2007/8
Source:
Studio:

The song grew out of a title that Gene simply liked as a phrase. According to Gene, this "Sonic Boom" era track was recorded, "as a trio. [Current KISS guitarist and drummer] Tommy Thayer, Eric Singer and myself. I had a track in mind, and we recorded it live, just the riff, and you'll hear me talking over it. Then I took it, and in my home studio, stuck on all the harmony parts, arranged it and put additional stuff on it. When other musicians aren't around, I wind up doing everything, whether it's keyboards or drums, if I can" (Ultimate Classic Rock, 11/14/2017). Gene later took the demo home to add the multi-layered harmonies.

He recalled, "That's all me in a home studio. I mean, if you know how those harmonies are stacked, then you can get that kind of blend. And that's not a high-fidelity quality recording, but you get the sense that if it was on a 72-track Neve board it would sound like Queen." According to Gene, the song was omitted from "Sonic Boom" due to being stylistically too similar to Paul's "Modern Day Delilah." This song is currently the only track to have been fully shared online legally, having been made freely available via SoundCloud in November 2017 to promote the Vault.

09. Hunger

(4:08) - Gene Simmons
Recorded: January 1986
Source:
Studio: Unknown Studio, Atlanta, GA

Gene recalled that this recording was cut around New Year's Eve 1985/86 in Atlanta, GA, where the band had played a show during the "Asylum" tour with a couple of days-off available before the first show of 1986. Recorded with Eric Carr and Bruce Kulick, this song might have been included in the batch of material Gene submitted for consideration for the "Crazy Nights" album. Amusingly, the song includes a break section very similar to "I Stole Your Love."

10. In My Head

(3:27) - Gene Simmons / Scott Van Zen / Jaime St. James

Recorded: 1993/4
Source: 16-track
Studio:
A 16-track demo recorded with an even darker vibe than the version recorded for the "Carnival of Souls" album.

11. Carnival of Souls #1

(3:38) - Gene Simmons / Scott Van Zen
Recorded: 1993/4
Source:
Studio:
This version of "Carnival of Souls" is similar, but not identical to the "Psycho Circus" out-take that surfaced in recent years. It shares the same general arrangement; including the "Passing Through" break section. It's not clear when it was recorded and with which players.

12. Are You a Boy, or Are You a Girl

(2:46) - Gene Simmons
Recorded: 1988?
Source:
Studio:
There isn't enough information to determine when this song was recorded or who the players were other than Gene and Tommy. This song bears no similarity to the 1966 Barbarians song with the same title, other than the title having inspired Gene to write a song of his own.

13. Say You Don't Want It

(3:24) - Gene Simmons
Recorded: 1997
Source:
Studio:
Appearance #1,232,999 of the "Daily Planet / Mongoloid Man" riff. Presumably, one day it will be included on a KISS album in some form! While in the liner notes Gene suggests that the song was demoed in 2001, he later mentions that it was recorded on the same day as "Just Gimme Love #2" in 1997 with Tommy Thayer on guitar.

14. Mongoloid Man

(3:58) - Gene Simmons
Recorded: 1978
Source:
Studio: Los Angeles, CA

Recorded with Joe Perry from Aerosmith and Michael Des Barres with falsetto backing vocals. Gene suggests that after having dinner with the members of Aerosmith he was going to return to the studio to continue working on ideas and Joe asked to play on the demo. The demo was based on the "Daily Planet" riff and had been described as a dance version of "War Machine" (Sharp, Ken - Goldmine). It's convenient that both Joe and Michael made guest appearances on Gene's 1978 solo album.

Gene has described some of the lyrics for the song, that were later recycled for use in "Spit," on the "Revenge" album: "I've got no manners and I'm not too clean / But I know what you like, if you know what I mean / I don't like to dress, I don't talk too good / 'Cause I'm a mongoloid man, it's understood // He's a mongoloid man / I do what I can / Mongoloid, a mongoloid / Mongoloid man" (Firehouse #68). Other lyrics were recycled for "Howling for Your Love" and for use in the "It Takes a Man like Me to Be a Woman like Me" piece for the "Never Too Young to Die" movie in 1986.

15. I Wait

(4:05) - Darren Leader / Gene Simmons
Recorded: 2002
Source:
Studio:

Based on a demo originally written by Steel Panther's drummer, who has also appeared on episodes of Gene Simmons Family Jewels (2007). Gene had announced on his website recording the demo of the song on April 25, 2002, planning to record a second song, "All the Kids with Painted

Faces" (see disk 9) a couple of weeks later. Further details are currently unknown. Dave Grohl on line 1...

Disk 02

Running time: 53:48

16. Weapons

(4:16) - Gene Simmons
Recorded: 1997
Source:
Studio:

The original demo of the song that later became "Weapons (Of Mass Destruction)" on Gene's 2004 "Asshole" album. This version starts with the main riff being played unamplified on an electric guitar. While not credited specifically, both Eric Singer and Bruce Kulick perform on the backing track. This song was under consideration for use on the 1998 "Psycho Circus" album.

17. Weapons (Power to Raise the Dead)

(4:12) - Gene Simmons / Ace Frehley
Recorded: 1998
Source:
Studio:

While Gene's "Weapons" was rejected for "Psycho Circus," he offered the song to Ace to sing. However, Ace didn't like the song's lyrics and instead rewrote it more to his liking. This version features Ace singing, to the original backing track.

18. Hate

(3:41) - Gene Simmons / Bruce Kulick / Scott Van Zen
Recorded: 1993/4
Source:
Studio:

This demo of the lead-off track off "Carnival of Souls" is illustrative of how much was lost in translation to finished product. While being of less multi-tracked demo quality, what it lacks in sonic fidelity it more than makes up for with its aggressive tone. In an interview with the Decibel Geek podcast, Scott described Gene as a master of making tape edits on demos they were working on in order to quickly change the arrangements (there's a good example of this at the end of "Hate").

19. Carnival of Souls #2
(3:15) - Gene Simmons / Scott Van Zen
Recorded: 1993
Source: 4-track
Studio:
The original demo of the unused title track from "Carnival of Souls," which was later revisited for KISS' "Psycho Circus." While the song eventually appeared on Gene's 2004 "Asshole" album, this version does not feature all the completed lyrics, though it includes the "Passing Through" break section. Scott plays bass and guitar with a drum machine being used for percussion. With the song originating in late-1993 it is likely that this demo dates from the following year.

20. Master of Flash ⊙
(3:37) - Jon Montgomery
Recorded: 1980
Source: 4-track
Studio: Home recording
According to a 1976 copyright registration, this song was written by members of Street Punk (Bobby Blain and Jon Montgomery), a band that KISS performed with during August 1973. The copyright was transferred to KISS in 1980 after Gene purchased the song, having decided after hearing it that it had to be *his* song. Jon released a solo version of the song on MySpace in 2009 and his "Through the Years" album in 2014. With lyrics such as "All the kids with painted faces follow him around, all the girls with satin and laces know when he's in town," it's hardly surprising that Gene found the song appealing. With its strutting very Bowie "Ziggy Stardust" style, it's a song Gene wishes he had written. For the demo, Gene recorded acoustic to 4-track with a guitar solo overdub. Another Street Punk song, "Rock

'n' Roll Appetite" is alleged to have been the basis for KISS' "Rock and Roll All Nite" and "Tomorrow and Tonight."

21. Heavy Rain

(3:24) - Gene Simmons / Bruce Kulick
Recorded: 1993/4
Source:
Studio:

Another re-write of "Rain Keeps Falling" with a heavier and bleaker tone; part of this song would be recycled as the bridge in "Within."

22. Within

(5:58) - Gene Simmons
Recorded: 1993/4
Source:
Studio:

This is the original "Carnival of Souls" era demo with Eric Singer and Bruce Kulick. This recording starts with Gene's recorded notes about the song before going into the backwards guitar intro.

23. In Your Face

(1:51) - Gene Simmons
Recorded: 1997
Source:
Studio:

Gene's original lo-fi demo of the "Psycho Circus" bonus track features strikingly different lyrics to the version Ace would later sing. Unfortunately, for whatever reason, this demo runs just 1:51, but provides enough evidence for contrast. Interestingly, during the KISS Kruise Vault presentation in 2017, Gene detailed using a loop of Eric Carr's "I Love It Loud" drum track for this demo.

24. In Your Face w/ Ace Frehley

(3:18) - Gene Simmons / Ace Frehley
Recorded: 1998

Source:
Studio:
Where Gene had wanted Ace to sing the song, Ace wasn't particularly keen on Gene's lyrics and rewrote them. This version of the recording is the same as one of the alternate takes that unofficially surfaced for collectors to enjoy in 2016.

25. Rain #2
(3:32) - Gene Simmons
Recorded: 1994
Source: 16-track
Studio:
Recorded with Eric Singer and Bruce Kulick, yet another rewrite of the "Rain Keeps Fallin'" idea.

26. Carnival (Intro)
(0:31) - Gene Simmons / Scott Van Zen
Recorded: 1993/4
Source:
Studio:
According to Gene, Scott Van Zen created this dark carnival intro at his behest using a public domain melody. In 1998 the original would be dumped out to 24-track to serve as the beginning of "Psycho Circus," though ultimately replaced with the more familiar final album version.

27. I Wanna Live
(4:33) - Gene Simmons / Vincent Cusano
Recorded: 1991
Source:
Studio: Chameleon Recording Studios, San Fernando, CA
This autobiographical piece is based around the idea of "All my father left me was his name." While "The Vault" notes are a bit muddled about this song — detailing the beginning of Gene's writing partnership with Vinnie (back in 1982), before moving into recording a demo of the song with members of Silent Rage — Vinnie has confirmed that it was one of the songs written for "Revenge." Additionally, Gene

has also mentioned that he and Vinnie worked on the instrumentation over a drumbeat created by the Silent Rage guys. This song recycles the riff from "Something Wicked This Way Comes" in the bridge. Vinnie's opinion of the song is simple: "I love that song."

28. If It's Too Hot, You're Too Cold

(3:41) - Gene Simmons
Recorded: 1990
Source:
Studio: Chameleon Recording Studios, San Fernando, CA
Gene has suggested that this song, later recycled for "Sonic Boom," was recorded with members of Silent Rage, placing its date in the early-1990s. That makes it yet another attempt to recycle elements of the ancient "Rotten to The Core" demo ...

29. Rain Keeps Fallin' #1 ✪

(3:22) - Gene Simmons
Recorded: 1991
Source:
Studio: Chameleon Recording Studios, San Fernando, CA
This version of "Rain Keeps Fallin'," the third version of this song on the disk, is a demo recorded with members of Silent Rage, who had been signed to Simmons' RCA distributed record label. Drums are via a drum machine and the overall quality of the recording is less polished than track 14 on the disk. Gene didn't give up on the track and it was re-recorded in 1998 and considered for the "Psycho Circus" album. This song was originally released on the deluxe "Gene Simmons Family Jewels" Season 1 DVD package in 2006. However, the arrangement is altered slightly, though some listeners may find the mastering of the 2006 version superior. Gene recycled the bass riff for "Without You I'm Nothing" on Ace Frehley's 2018 album "Spaceman."

30. Bells of Freedom

(4:37) - Gene Simmons

Recorded: 1997
Source:
Studio:

Dating from the 1990's this demo features a pre-KISS Tommy Thayer on guitar. Sounds like the same drummer as providing the count in on "Just Gimme Love #2.

(Fan made commemorative picks were made for most "Vault" Experience events)

Disk 03
Running time: 50:03

31. Christine Sixteen
(2:39) - Gene Simmons
Recorded: April 1977
Source:
Studio: Village Recorder Studios, Los Angeles, CA

Written while Gene was staying at the Sunset Marquis, this demo was recorded shortly after KISS' return from their Japan tour. Alex and Edward Van Halen were recruited for drums and guitars respectively when Gene decided to record the demos one evening during a session that only took a few hours. What is missing from the demo is the spoken word section, but otherwise the overall arrangement is the same. Anyone expecting a VH/KISS hybrid will be sadly disappointed, but another misconception can be put to rest: The piano pump is present on the song even at this early stage.

According to Gene, "We cut it live as a trio and Eddie came up with some solos afterwards. I liked his solo for 'Christine Sixteen' so much that when the band recorded it for 'Love Gun,' Ace pretty much copied Eddie's solo note-for-note" (KISStory). What he fails to mention is that it took Edward numerous takes to find the suitable simplistic solo that Gene was demanding; only after David Lee Roth had translated Gene's description into something Edward could relate to. And yes, Frehley's solo does mimic Eddie's original. The Vault book erroneously credits this song to the "Rock and Roll Over" album. It also includes a picture of the 10" single acetate which was erroneously labeled "demo."

32. Tunnel of Love

(3:31) - Gene Simmons
Recorded: April 1977
Source:
Studio: Village Recorder Studios, Los Angeles, CA
Following the same overall arrangement as the recording on his 1978 solo album, this demo is more notable for the Edward Van Halen guitar solo. Minor lyrical changes are present with "You'll jump off the roof if I say / I won't let you get away" being made more child friendly the following year. Notes suggest that Gene had written this song in Osaka in March 1977 during the Japan tour.

33. Have Love Will Travel

(3:10) - Gene Simmons
Recorded: April 1977
Source:
Studio: Village Recorder Studios, Los Angeles, CA
"Have Love Will Travel" later became "Got Love for Sale" on the "Love Gun" album. The Vault book incorrectly gives it that later title, with it even having been referred by the original title in the KISS Army newsletter. After many years of wanting to release the VH demos, it took a relatively simple deal to facilitate Edward's agreement. Gene gave Edward the original 24-track masters of the 15 demos he

recorded of the band in 1976, during the brief period he was (unsuccessfully) involved in trying to get the band signed.

34. Hell or High Water
(3:10) - Gene Simmons / Bruce Kulick
Recorded: 1986
Source: 4-track
Studio: Home
This demo is further proof that "Crazy Nights" could have been a far better album without the production polishing that was forced upon the material. Even in rougher form, due to being recorded at Bruce's condo, Gene's sense of melody comes through.

35. Domino ✪
(3:46) - Gene Simmons
Recorded: 1991
Source: 8-track
Studio: Chameleon Recording Studios, San Fernando, CA
Demoed with members of Silent Rage, plus a drum machine, this track was previously released on the 2001 KISS "Box Set." However, the Vault version is clearly tempo adjusted with an edited outro section that shortens the arrangement. Sounds better down a half-step.

36. Mad Dog ✪
(2:27) - Gene Simmons
Recorded: 1975
Source:
Studio: Magna Graphic Studios, New York City
One of several demos recorded in the summer of 1975 in preparation for the album that would become "Destroyer." JR Smalling is credited on drums this time, unlike when the song was included on the KISS "Box Set" in 2001. And while this is the same version as the earlier release it is a substantially improved master.

37. Only You
(4:34) - Gene Simmons

Recorded: 1979
Source:
Studio:

A striking example of the benefit of Bob Ezrin's input on material, this demo revamped his far earlier "Eskimo Sun," but only the verses bear any resemblance to the "Elder" version making it an almost uncomfortable listen, though the recording does feature some exquisite lead guitar work by an uncredited guitar player.

38. True Confessions #2

(3:33) - Gene Simmons
Recorded: 1978
Source: 24-track
Studio: Record Plant Studios, New York City

Several versions of this song are included on the Vault. This 24-track recording features prominent backing vocals by the "Group with No Name," an act signed to Casablanca that included Katey Sagal ("Married with Children"), Franny Eisenberg, and Carolyn Ray. Gene had met Katey at The Great American Food and Beverage Company and discovered that he'd gone to school with one of her band members. As a result, he put them in touch with Neil Bogart. This version closely mirrors Gene's solo album version's arrangement.

39. Childhood's End

(3:32) - Gene Simmons / Bruce Kulick / Tommy Thayer
Recorded: 1993
Source:
Studio:

Substantially different to the "Carnival of Souls" version with music and arrangement, and a fair number of pinch harmonics. As a result, the demo seems almost completely different to the song that most will be familiar with.

40. Burning Up with Fever #2

(3:05) - Gene Simmons
Recorded: 1976/77

Source:
Studio: Magna Graphic Studios, New York City
Having been demoed with KISS at Larrabee Studios in Los Angeles in January 1975, and again in July of that year with JR Smalling on drums, this later demo is still a song in search of a purpose.

41. Good Girl Gone Bad
(4:04) - Gene Simmons / Davitt Sigerson
Recorded: 1986
Source:
Studio:
It's curious why Peter Diggins' writing credit is removed from the Vault version. Whatever the case, this demo closely follows the form that would be recorded for the "Crazy Nights" album, but lacking the polished production gives the song a fuller character. Fans of Bruce Kulick's guitar playing will enjoy the raw tone of his lead work and the solo on this piece. The demo is backed by a drum machine.

42. Live Fast, Die Young
(3:32) - Gene Simmons / Bruce Kulick
Recorded: 1985
Source:
Studio:
It might be obtuse to suggest that this demo is incorrectly titled as "Trial by Fire" on the Vault, but the song's original title was well known to have been "Live Fast Die Young." The chorus of the demo provides more than adequate evidence that the lyrical transformation into the "Asylum" song had not yet occurred. Many Vault purchasers may not be versed in the arcane minutiae that consume some... That being said, it is only really the chorus that varies from the version of the song recorded for "Asylum," and it is clear that this original really didn't work that well.

43. Secretly Cruel

(3:46) - Gene Simmons
Recorded: 1983
Source:
Studio:

This version of Gene's demo is not one of a pair (the other being "Any Way You Slice It") that have circulated for decades for collectors that were recorded for the "Asylum" album. However, like that earlier demo it is clear that recording on a vintage Tascam tape recorder, which Gene suggests was dated 1981, didn't provide the highest fidelity in the first place. This version is closer to the finished album version of the song, though lacks a guitar solo (which is present on the previously circulating demo).

44. Love 'Em and Leave 'Em Yeah

(2:18) - Gene Simmons
Recorded: 1976
Source:
Studio:

An earlier version of the song that would be included on "Rock and Roll Over," this demo has circulated in lower quality for decades with the title "Rock and Rolls Royce." It provides another example of the transitions Gene's ideas undergo in the song writing process recycling the part of the original "Drive Me Wild" demo, which had been replaced by Paul's lyrics during its transition into "Rock and Roll All Nite." The free-form guitar solo indicates that Ace, or perhaps Binky Phillips, may have contributed, though that's not confirmed. Parts of the guitar structure of the song later became "Sweet Pain," while the riff from the chorus was later used on "Burn Bitch Burn." Waste not, want not.

45. Am I Losing My Mind

(2:55) - Gene Simmons
Recorded: 1980
Source:
Studio:

Recycling the main chords to "Only You" with other parts of "Eskimo Sun," Gene created this dance song backed with a disco beat. It provides another interesting look at Simmons' willingness to embrace anything, and then walk away from it and start over!

Disk 04

Running time: 51:10

46. Plaster Caster ✪

(3:34) - Gene Simmons
Recorded: 1977
Source:
Studio: Electric Lady, New York City, NY

Previously released on the KISS "Love Gun" deluxe album in 2015, this version is a different master that some fans may find superior. The tempo is stretched slightly. With the amount of bonus material Gene contributed to that product it is hardly surprising that his personal Vault still has a lot of material left in it, even with this release! Gene recalled recording this demo in the dead of night and performing all the instruments, including drums, himself.

47. X-Ray Eyes

(3:41) - Gene Simmons
Recorded: 1978
Source:
Studio: Planet Studios, Los Angeles, CA

Gene performed all the instruments on this demo. Inspired by Superman's power to see through objects, the God of Thunder could instead see through your lies!

48. Charisma

(3:17) - Gene Simmons / Howard Marks
Recorded: 1978
Source:
Studio:

Howard Marks' background included writing jingles with Sean Delaney for their Music Department Company. This jingle background gave birth to the song, according to Gene, "He jotted down a few lines I liked. 'What is ma? Charisma. ... and so on.' I wrote the song around a few of his lines" (GeneSimmons.com). Gene would recycle Wicked Lester's "Simple Type" chordal structure for the song.

49. Rockin' in the U.S.A.

(2:53) - Gene Simmons
Recorded: 1977
Source:
Studio:
Gene performed all the instruments on this demo, which features a slightly different arrangement to that which was recorded for the studio side of "Alive II."

50. Radioactive ✪

(3:04) - Gene Simmons
Recorded: 1977
Source:
Studio:
Previously released on the 2001 KISS "Box Set." This version of the song features a different master with shortened intro. The demo features the Group with No Name girls, including Katey Sagal, on backing vocals.

51. See You in Your Dreams Tonight

(2:17) - Gene Simmons
Recorded: 1977
Source:
Studio: Record Plant, New York City, NY
Originally written in March 1976, Gene performed all the instruments on this demo, which also features the Group with No Name girls on backing vocals. Those vocals were added a year after the demo was originally recorded as Gene started thinking about re-recording the song on his solo album

52. Man of 1,000 Faces #1

(2:48) - Gene Simmons
Recorded: 1976
Source:
Studio: Record Plant Studios, New York City, NY
Written in Oct. 1974, Gene performed all the instruments on this demo recording. Vocals are delivered in an almost narrative style with striking enunciation. Handwritten lyrics

on Evansville, IN, Holiday Inn stationary certainly makes it plausible that the song was written on the road around the date Gene noted on the different lyrics appearing in "The Vault" book. Interestingly, lyrics for "Almost Human" are written on the other side of the sheet...

53. Man of 1,000 Faces #2 ✶
(2:54) - Gene Simmons
Recorded: July 1975
Source: 8-Track
Studio: Magna Graphic Studios, New York City, NY
A second version of the song recorded with Ace on guitar and JR Smalling on drums. Gene suggests that he didn't like this version and went back into the studio (Record Plant) to re-record it. This version is an edit, and the complete recording (3:33 duration) was released on the KISS "45th Anniversary Super Deluxe Edition" of "Destroyer" in 2021. It restores an edited middle section and allows the song to run longer rather than the early fade that ends this version.

54. Calling Dr. Love
(2:50) - Gene Simmons
Recorded: 1976
Source:
Studio:
Recorded with an unnamed studio drummer, the form of the song had reached that which KISS recorded for "Rock and Roll Over."

55. Bad, Bad Lovin' / Calling Dr. Love ✪ ✶
(3:03) - Gene Simmons
Recorded: July 1975
Source: 8-Track
Studio: Magna Graphic Studios, New York City, NY
A version of the song recorded with Ace on guitar and JR Smalling on drums. This recording is the same as the 2001 "Box Set" version, albeit with the ending section shortened by starting the fade-out earlier. The "Box Set" version was

also included, with improved mastering, on the KISS "45th Anniversary Super Deluxe Edition" of "Destroyer" in 2021.

56. Almost Human
(3:19) - Gene Simmons
Recorded:
Source:
Studio:
Written in April 1976, Gene again played all the instruments on this recording. The form is nearly identical to that later recorded by KISS.

57. Burning Up with Fever #1 ✶
(3:18) - Gene Simmons
Recorded: July 1975
Source: 8-Track
Studio: Magna Graphic Studios, New York City, NY
Having first recorded the song with KISS at Larrabee Studios in Los Angeles, in Jan. 1975, Gene wasn't happy with the result. As a result, the tempo is taken down and the song made less poppy and more menacing. It was recorded again during preparations for the "Destroyer" album, this recording purportedly features Gene on all the instruments (other than drums — which were performed by JR Smalling).

This version appears to be a bit of a hatchet job of the circulating demo, at ~0:56 in there are hints of a cut 'n' paste from section later in the song where the solo section begins, particularly for the last line of the chorus which replaced growl leading into the vocal of the third verse. the complete recording was released on the KISS "45th Anniversary Super Deluxe Edition" of "Destroyer" in 2021.

58. True Confessions #1 ✶
(3:24) - Gene Simmons
Recorded: July 1975
Source: 8-Track
Studio: Magna Graphic Studios, New York City, NY

While Gene suggests that this demo features the Group with No Name girls on backing vocals, it instead is the original recording dating to prior to the "Destroyer" sessions and includes JR Smalling on drums. Unlike the circulating version that faded out soon after the guitar solo the full song is represented, albeit in mono. The KISS "45th Anniversary Super Deluxe Edition" of "Destroyer" presents a full stereo version of the track.

59. Goin' Blind / Little Lady
(3:04) - Gene Simmons / Stephen Coronel
Recorded: 1970
Source: 2-track reel
Studio: Brooke's Nutley, NJ Living Room
Likely another of the tracks recorded with Brooke Ostrander on keys for use on Gene's 12 song demo reel (presumably he retained a copy which had 1 side with the material recorded at 3 3/4 and the other at 7 1/2 IPS, or the original 13 track compilation). This version of the song features the original "Little Lady from the land beneath the sea" lyric and lacks Paul Stanley's later contribution of "I'm 93 and you're 16."

60. Larger Than Life
(3:56) - Gene Simmons
Recorded: 1977
Source:
Studio:
Gene again plays all the instruments on this recording. The form is nearly identical to that recorded by KISS for the "Alive II" album, apart from the spoken ending section.

61. It's My Life ⊙
(3:48) - Gene Simmons / Paul Stanley
Recorded: 1982
Source:
Studio: Record Plant Studios, Los Angeles, CA
The same as the long circulating demo recording, though this version has the intro drum section shortened slightly.

Unfortunately, audio brick-walling prevents fans from enjoying the crystal-clear version they were hoping for. This song was first performed live by the Gene Simmons Band on Feb. 16, 2018 at the Lynn Auditorium in Lynn, MA. Unfortunately, Gene has erroneously suggested that the song grew out of an abandoned Paul Stanley demo, "Every Little Piece of My Heart," from "The Elder" era. That is not the case, with that Paul Stanley idea piece ultimately becoming "A World without Heroes," with Gene's input and the assistance of Lou Reed. Ultimately, the basis of "It's My Life" was Paul Stanley's, and when he opted to not pursue it Gene completed the song based on Paul's melody and pre-existing chorus.

Disk 05

Running time: 60:04

62. See You Tonite

(2:29) - Gene Simmons
Recorded: 197?
Source:
Studio:

A crystal-clear version of the demo that has circulated for many years. Song one on "The Best of Gene Simmons," this song was written prior to Wicked Lester at Steve Coronel's grandfather's house yet had not been included on Gene's 1970 publishing demo. Very little changed between the demo and Gene's 1978 recording, except the second line of the song being changed from "Don't know if I'll ever find it, but now" to "I don't have any doubts about that fact."

63. You're My Reason #2

(3:23) - Gene Simmons
Recorded: 1976
Source:
Studio:

This acoustic flavored original demo features Gene on all instruments and multiple layers of vocals. Slower tempo it is more a vehicle for the more complete verses. If the recoding date of this song is truly prior to "Christine Sixteen" then Gene clearly liked a good piano pump, even at that time.

64. Always Near You

(2:57) - Gene Simmons
Recorded: 197?
Source:
Studio:

Inspired by the ghost story "The Ghost and Mrs. Muir" (a 1947 movie and TV series that ran 1968–1970), this song would later be reinterpreted for Gene's 1978 solo album. Gene plays all the instruments on this demo but is joined by

Nancy Parkinson on backing vocals. While Gene suggests that there are no drums in the liner notes, there are...

65. One More Chance

(3:12) - Gene Simmons
Recorded: 197?
Source:
Studio:

An earlier demo containing parts (primarily the verses) that would be recycled into "Mr. Make Believe" on Gene's 1978 solo album. Gene performs all the instrumentation on the demo.

66. Now That You're Gone #2 Synth

(2:47) - Gene Simmons / Robert Kulick
Recorded: 2000
Source:
Studio:

Sonically, it seems likely that the descriptions in the Vault book were swapped around for this version and song #72. Inspired by a "Garth Brooks Does KISS" spoof Gene heard on the radio while on the "Farewell" tour with KISS, he tracked down those participants to see what they could do with this song as he was planning to include it on his Sanctuary Records solo album. With keyboards and drum machine the song's pop sensibilities remain very much intact. Gene recalled, "Jeff Diehl, a guy from Indiana, did the rest. He sent me a tape of what Garth Brooks or the Beatles would sound like doing KISS songs. I heard this, loved it, [and] asked if he wanted to try a track. By phone I told him how I wanted it to sound" (Gene Simmons PR).

67. You're My Reason for Living Synth ✪

(4:16) - Gene Simmons
Recorded: 1991–93
Source:
Studio:

Many fans will have already heard this track, with it previously having originally been released in 2003 on Gene

Simmons' "Sex Money KISS" audio lunchbox bonus disk and Japanese "Asshole" release; the synth version on the "Vault" has a slightly different arrangement of the same general music track removing the second verse "I Was Lonely" for a 4:17 length versus the original 4:22. Recorded with members of Silent Rage. According to Jesse Damon (the band's singer/guitarist), the song demo was "recorded sometime between 1991–93. Around 10 years ago. I absolutely thought it was a smash hit, not our demo, I mean the song itself, the chorus 'You're My Reason for Livin,' says it all." Damon would release a stripped back version of the song on his 2004 album "Nothin' Else Matters."

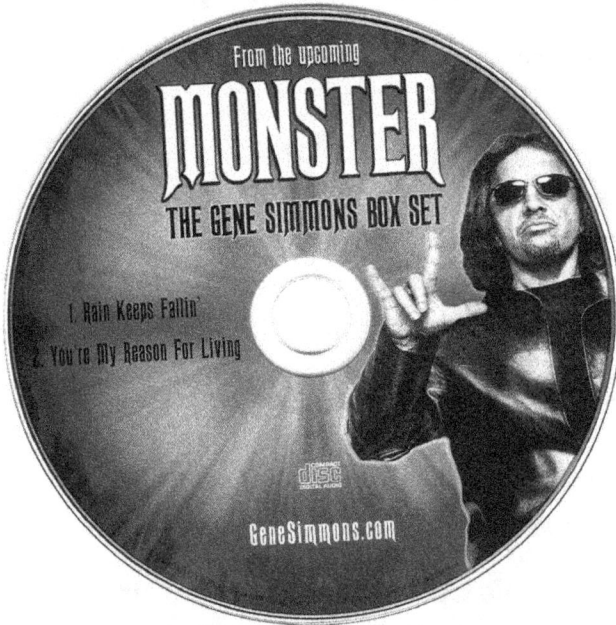

68. Dreamer
(3:02) - Gene Simmons
Recorded: 1976
Source:
Studio:

In terms of its historic importance to Gene's development as a songwriter this track might otherwise be ignored. It is based on two separate ancient Simmons compositions,

"When I Awoke" (4:15 length) and "Something of a Dreamer," the former of which was included on his 1970 12-song 7" publishing demo reel. The verse comes from the former, but as Gene recounts in the liner notes, he was recycling various ideas into a new piece while writing with a 12-string guitar in his kitchen. Roughly 20 seconds of the original demo has been removed through starting the fade-out early, to reduce the repetitiveness of the ending.

69. Na, Na, Na, Na
(2:47) - Bob Dylan / Gene Simmons
Recorded: 1991
Source:
Studio: Cherokee Studios

A variation on the chords that Gene and Bob came up with during their writing session, with the vocals being far more scat illustrating the beginnings of an idea that would ultimately become "Waiting for The Morning Light." Gene recalled writing with Bob: "Like anything else, it's out there and you can reach for it or not. And one of the things I had in mind was to write with Bob Dylan, no matter how silly or impossible that sounds. It was no different than writing by myself or anybody else, except when he walked in the room — 'Oh my God, this guy's written some of the great songs of the century!'" (Scripps Howard News Service, 1/3/93).

At the Los Angeles Vault experience Steve Genewick, who had been a third engineer at Cherokee Studios, reminisced about Gene and Bob recording a session together at that studio in 1991. Tommy Thayer recalled, "One day I got a call from Gene and he says, 'Get a drummer and a keyboard player and meet me down at Cherokee Studios at 7pm tonight, we're going to record a song I wrote with Bob Dylan.' I'm like, 'wow, seriously?' I brought my Les Paul and two acoustic guitars, a 6 and a 12-string that I borrowed from my buddy Marc Ferrari. I get there and sure enough in walks Bob Dylan and his girlfriend. Suddenly I'm thinking, 'it's Bob Dylan, the guy who influenced the Beatles and Jimi

Hendrix, unreal.' He says, 'let me show you the chord changes,' and we proceed to pass the 12-string acoustic back and forth. It seemed like one of the most surreal things I've ever experienced" (Coffee Talk [with Tommy Thayer]).

70. Mr. Make Believe
(2:27) - Gene Simmons
Recorded: 1977
Source: 4-track
Studio: "Primitive 4-track studio in a very seedy part of Detroit."
Recorded in Detroit on a day off while on tour, sometime after January 1977. This demo provided the basic music for "One More Chance," though the "Mr. Make Believe" is the key component with Gene trying to write a song with a similar message of "When You Wish upon a Star." Again, Gene plays all the instruments and provides his own vocal harmonies.

71. Now That You're Gone #3
(3:52) - Gene Simmons / Robert Kulick
Recorded: 1988
Source:
Studio: Fortress Studio, Los Angeles, CA
A heavier reinterpretation of the song with Kevin Valentine on drums and Tommy Thayer on guitars. Engineered by Pat Regan. However, sonically, this song may well date from 1997 as the process of it becoming two different songs commenced.

72. Now That You're Gone #1
(3:38) - Gene Simmons / Robert Kulick
Recorded: 1977
Source: 4-track
Studio:
Sonically, it seems likely that the descriptions in the Vault book were swapped around for this version and song #66. Gene suggests that this song was based on the structure of Bowie's "All the Young Dudes," with Bob Kulick performing the guitar. Lyrically, it was very much autobiographical.

Light synth is added to piece, as are the children choir section and vocal call outs making it more plaintive. Originally written in 1977 by Gene and Bob Kulick. Parts of the song would be updated while Gene was recording it for his "Asshole" album in 2003.

73. You're My Reason for Living 4-Track

(3:43) - Gene Simmons
Recorded: 1980
Source: 4-track
Studio:

The demo's title says it all, being Gene's 4-track demo of the song. With no drums and Gene performing all other instruments, with numerous over-dubs, this was Gene's second attempt to paint the sonic tapestry of the song. The guitar solo cuts at 2:41 suggesting either an awkward 4-track edit or removal of a section of the original source as the song heads back into the verse.

74. We Are One

(3:03) - Gene Simmons
Recorded: 199?
Source:
Studio:

Gene suggests that this song was demoed with members of Silent Rage, which would date it to the early 1990s. At this stage of development, he clearly has the basic melody and some lyrics, but there are numerous scat sections where he doesn't yet have the words. The chorus is well is defined, as is the bridge. It would still take several rewrites of this song (in 1997) before it reached an arrangement that Gene was satisfied with for use on the "Psycho Circus" album.

75. Everybody Wants Somebody

(2:40) - Bob Dylan / Gene Simmons
Recorded: 1991
Source:
Studio:

Another effort using the chord patterns Gene had worked on with Bob Dylan, with Tommy Thayer on acoustic guitar. Very much a low-fidelity "demo" — it's the basic ideas being captured.

76. Bob Dylan Writing Session
(15:48) - Bob Dylan / Gene Simmons
Recorded: Sept. 23, 1991
Source:
Studio: Gene's house

Two legends chatting and bouncing ideas around. Surreal pop culture music history. Bob asking, "What else ya got?" is priceless. This may not be a track that remains in most fans' "Vault" play lists, but the discussion of styles of music and ideas allow fans to be a fly on the wall. Gene recalled, "Sitting down and writing songs with one of the classic writers of all time was unbelievable. The biggest lesson is, how normal he was."

Disk 06

Running time: 46:38

77. Waiting for the Morning Light

(3:53) - Bob Dylan / Gene Simmons
Recorded: 2002
Source:
Studio: Bag's Living Room, Vancouver, BC, Canada

The fully realized song that resulted from Gene and Bob Dylan's 1991 writing session was recorded for Gene's 2004 "Asshole" album. This is the third version of the album track to be released, with the first being the 3:46 "pre-release mix" having been released first on a European sampler EP (Sanctuary/Simmons Records SANPX-245), followed by the 3:22 album version. Like the difference between the two previous versions, sections are moved around or extended, but all based upon the same source.

Gene recalled Bag's input: "He basically took my demo and arranged it. There's nothing on there, besides keyboards, keyboard bass and sampled drums. There's not a guitar lick on the whole thing. Those piano melody lines were things that I came up with. It reminded me of a version of a melody I heard while I was growing up, a song called 'Black Orpheus' and also, 'Lara's Theme' from Doctor Zhivago and funnily enough the theme song from the TV series, Lassie" (Gene Simmons PR). Bag plays all of the instrumentation on the demo.

78. Is It Real

(0:59) - Gene Simmons
Recorded: 2009
Source:
Studio: Gene's kitchen

The song is introduced with Gene speaking out the chords while strumming an acoustic, E-A♭-G♭-B, serves as an introduction to the following track which developed out of the idea.

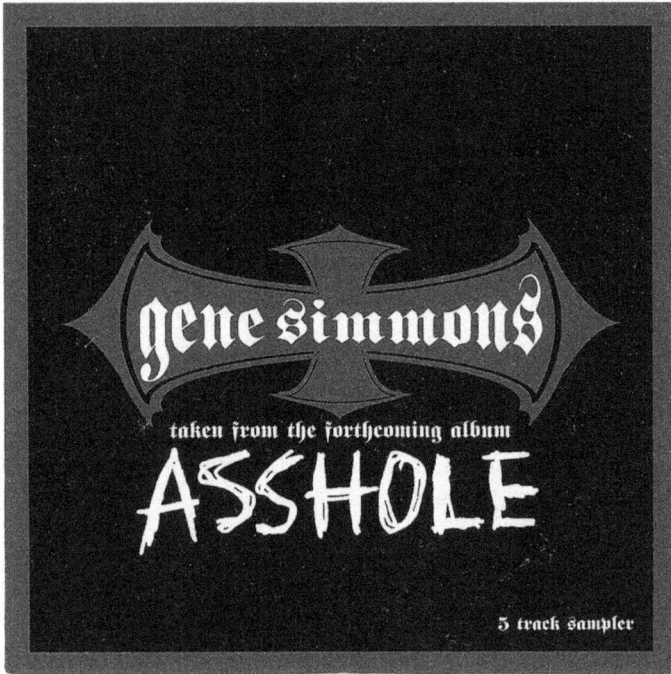

79. Are You Real
(2:48) - Gene Simmons
Recorded: 2011
Source:
Studio: Conway Recording Studios Studio C, Hollywood, CA
Fully realized development of the previous track recorded with Eric Singer and Tommy Thayer. Lyrically the song is based on the idea of a dream sometimes resulting in one wondering whether it was real or not.

80. Something Seems to Happen at Night
(2:36) - Adam Mitchell
Recorded: 1982
Source:
Studio:
This song is based on a bed-track that was recorded solely by Adam Mitchell, which he simply asked Gene to sing the

lyrics to. Gene simply liked the song's vibe, which is more laid back and stylistically different to the usual sort of material he generates. The song was the first of Adam's compositions that he ever played for Gene. He recalled, "The first song I ever played for him when he came over to my house was a song I had written separately by myself called 'Something Seems to Happen at Night.' I'd written the entire song. Gene liked it so he sang a vocal to it."

81. I Believe

(2:32) - Gene Simmons
Recorded: 201?
Source: ProTools
Studio: Gene's House

Using the same chord pattern as "Is It Real" and "Are You Real," Gene updated the song with engineer Erich Lenning on a ProTools setup. Erich was the engineer responsible for the transfers of many of the songs appearing on the Vault. Lyrically, Gene was looking for a big declaratory intent with a large dose of inspiration from the Beatles.

82. Beautiful ⊙

(3:45) - Mark Addison / Nina Singh
Recorded: 2002
Source:
Studio: Aerie Studio, Austin, TX

Written by members of the band "Kitty Gordon," from Austin, Texas, this song had originally been released with the title "Somebody Beautiful" on the band's 1999 debut EP "Seven." It was also included on the band's full album "Weather" in 2001. According to Gene, "this was one of those story songs, the lyrics killed me. It had this kind of pan-sexual, 'Lola' (The Kinks) flavor to it, and also a kind of pathos. He's a poor guy, who's six foot four in his six-inch heels, a cupid tattoo behind his ear, 'spends all his money on silicone honey,' those lyrics are just classic" (Gene Simmons PR). This version is simply Gene's vocals over the original Kitty Gordon track which would later be enhanced for use on Gene's "Asshole" album.

83. Guilty Pleasures

(2:53) - Gene Simmons
Recorded: 2011
Source:
Studio: Conway Recording Studios Studio C, Hollywood, CA

Recorded with Eric Singer and Tommy Thayer this song was written on an acoustic guitar while Gene wintered in Whistler, Canada with Shannon. Being in Canada, Gene was impressed by Neil Young's use of minor chords married to a confessional lyric.

84. I Dream 1,000 Dreams

(3:35) - Gene Simmons
Recorded: Aug. 31, 1998
Source:
Studio:

Gene is proud that this unusual song is the only one that he has ever written that came to him fully formed — he woke up with the melody any lyrically, before even knowing what the chords would be. This demo is the basis for the more concise "Asshole" album version without elements such as additional orchestral and steel guitar overdubs.

85. I Am Yours #1

(4:02) - Gene Simmons
Recorded: 1997/8
Source:
Studio:

It's pretty clear that there are strong similarities between this version and the "Psycho Circus" out-take that has circulated in recent years. Likely from digital source the arrangement has been tightened up and combined with proper mastering for proper presentation. Gene suggests in the Vault book that members of Silent Rage were the backing group on this song, but it seems more likely that

Tommy Thayer was involved in this version. Gene's inspiration for this song was David Bowie's "All the Young Dudes."

86. I Am Yours #2

(4:24) - Gene Simmons
Recorded:
Source:
Studio:
Gene's original demo is likely the version recorded with members of Silent Rage in the early 1990s.

87. Love Is Blind #1 ⊙

(2:51) - Gene Simmons
Recorded: 1977
Source:
Studio:
This song was originally released on the 2001 KISS "Box Set," though the Vault version features a slightly different arrangement. The song was written on the road in 1977 and was recorded on a day off with Gene providing all the instrumentation. According to Gene, "I recorded that song on the road (possibly Chattanooga, Tenn.) about 1977. I used a click track for drums, one electric guitar and one bass. I sang all the vocals and harmonies" (GeneSimmons.com). With the original song lyrics having been written on Sheraton Inn-Abilene stationary, and Gene's comments about possibly recording it in Tennessee, it would seem possible that the song dates from November 1977 due to the tour routing at the time.

88. Love Is Blind #2

(4:12) - Gene Simmons
Recorded:
Source: 4-track
Studio:
An attempt by Gene to take the original song and "beef" it up with a different treatment of the guitars. There's a very awkward section at 2:32 to incorporate a drum break.

89. Whatever Turns You On
(3:02) - Dave Williams / Gene Simmons
Recorded:
Source:
Studio:

A song from another band that submitted a demo to Simmons Records, this recording features Gene's partner Shannon Tweed and her mother on the gang backing vocals. According to Gene, "When I first told people on my web site... to send in demos, I received close to 5,000 demos. 'Whatever Turns You On' came to me as one of those demos. It didn't have that title. I contacted Dave Williams, the lead singer of the band who wrote it. I called him, told him I was interested in the track, and changed it around a little, changed the title, it was my chorus idea and I rewrote some of the lyrics. The musical track is Dave and his band. Singing background is Miss Shannon Tweed, and her mother, Louise and a friend of theirs" (Gene Simmons PR). Released on Gene's 2004 "Asshole" album, this is purportedly the demo of the track.

90. Hold On
(2:52) - Gene Simmons
Recorded:
Source:
Studio:

Based loosely on "Love Is Blind," particularly the chorus, Gene wrote this song while visiting Shannon's mother in Canada. The backing band is comprised of members of Silent Rage.

91. First Love
(2:14) - Gene Simmons
Recorded: 201?
Source: ProTools
Studio: Gene's House

Demoed the day after "I Believe," this song was originally written by Gene in the 1970s on piano but does reuse some of the melody from "Now That You're Gone." Sophie

Simmons recorded a version of the song as part of an episode of Gene Simmons Family Jewels in 2008.

Disk 07

Running time: 50:29

92. No Conscience
(3:32) - Gene Simmons / Vini Poncia
Recorded: 1988
Source:
Studio:
Gene's Vault book is very light on the details concerning this track, other than giving an overview of Vini's history working with KISS. The general melody was transformed into "Love's A Slap in the Face" on the "Hot in the Shade" album marking it as a prototype. Lyrically, the demo was based on a conversation between the two when they sat down and started writing together. It's also pretty clear Bruce Kulick is featured on guitar.

93. Suspicious ⊙
(3:18) - Tommy Thayer / Jaime St. James / Pat Regan
Recorded: 1987
Source:
Studio:
This recording is Gene's vocal take of a song that appeared on Black 'N' Blue's final Geffen album, "In Heat," in 1988. The band were trying to combine ideas such as Stevie Wonder's "I Ain't Superstitious" and the chorus of the Bee Gee's "Stayin' Alive" for a radio accessible song. However, only one single ("Live It Up") would be released in support of the album. The backing track does not appear to be the same as the version used by Black 'N' Blue, though that band's voices are clearly present on the backgrounds. This song formed part of the audio montage used to promote the Vault.

94. Everybody Wants ⊙
(2:23) - Gene Simmons / Jesse Damon
Recorded: 1991
Source:

Studio:
According to co-writer Jesse Damon, "This was the first song Gene and I wrote together; it was in the running as a song for a possible KISS album but didn't make it. I liked it so much, years later I recorded it, and put it out on my solo CD! When we wrote the song, it came together very easy. I remember it taking only a couple sessions to write it, and knew this was a good experience for both Gene and I. I thought to myself this is the beginning of a great writing relationship" (JG). Jesse would release his recording of the song on his "The Hand That Rocks" solo album in 2002. Originally titled "Everybody Wants Somebody," Gene shortened the title on the Vault due to the Dylan track with a similar title. Mark Hawkins plays guitar on the track.

95. Promise the Moon
(3:55) - Gene Simmons / Robert Kulick / Tommy Thayer / Jamie St. James
Recorded: 1986
Source:
Studio:
Based on the main riff of one of several unrealized "Elder" instrumentals, this song had been recorded by Black 'N Blue for their 1986 "Nasty, Nasty" album (it remained listed in the performance credits with keyboards being performed by John Purdell). However, it was dropped at the last minute in favor of the more commercial Jonathan Cain penned "I'll Be There for You." In fact, Gene dates it to the 1970s where it began life as a collaboration with Bob Kulick, then titled "Sentimental Fool." One will also notice that much of the melody is similar to that used in parts on the "Rain Keeps Fallin'" demo. Waste not, want not...

96. All You Want's a Piece of My Heart
(3:51) - Adam Mitchell
Recorded: 1988
Source:
Studio:

This track is simply Gene singing one of Adam's songs with Tommy Thayer on guitar and background vocals. From the folks involved this recording likely dates from the "In Heat" era of Black 'N' Blue when Adam was involved in co-writing with Jamie and Tommy.

97. Pride ⊙
(3:06) - Matt McCormack / Gene Simmons
Recorded: 2003
Source:
Studio: Slaughterhouse Studios, Austin, TX

Has had been the case with "Beautiful," this song had also come to Gene through his cattle-call for material for his planned re-launch of Simmons Records — or perhaps more accurately as his search for new outside collaborators and/or material. The original "Pride" had a basis very much more rooted in the "downhearted, slower and very Mississippi Delta blues meets Chris Robinson from the Black Crowes" (Artist Waves) according to Matt. It was an idea he and previous college band member had had, though Gene gravitated towards the subject matter of the song. Ultimately, Gene couldn't make the song work for his solo album, and Matt released it on his "Life in Stereo" album in August 2017.

98. Mirage ⊙
(3:27) - Gene Simmons
Recorded: 1988
Source:
Studio:

Most fans will be aware of the Doro version of this song released on her 1990 album produced by Gene. However, we now learn that it developed out of a 1970s song titled "Through the Night," and a later Stanley/Simmons collaboration titled "Sweetheart of the Radio." Unfortunately, while the liner notes suggest that both those precursors are included on the Vault, they weren't. Perhaps on Vault II... Gene explained at the Nashville Vault

Experience that he written for Doro because she couldn't really write. Another song written for the project, "Unholy Love," became the seed for KISS' "Unholy" the following year which Gene had a basic idea for that benefitted from the input and refinements of Vinnie Vincent.

99. Dog

(3:31) - Alex Chuaqui / Gene Simmons
Recorded: 2002
Source:
Studio: Bag's Living Room, Vancouver, BC, Canada

Written by Gene Simmons and Bag (who also arranged the piece), who just happened to be the first act signed to Simmons Records. Gene has previously commented, "'Dog' was mostly written by Bag. It was recorded in bag's living room. Bag played all the instruments. He's also singing harmonies on the song. Bag also sings the Warren Zevon sounding 'Werewolves of London' vocal part. I wanted to make the song longer and remembered the Sam the Sham and The Pharaohs song, 'Little Red Riding Hood.' That's where I came up with the howling part in the beginning. In that song it struck me as the wolf talking to the little girl, it was very sexual. So, I did that spoken word interlude, 'what a big tongue you got, the better to eat you with, my dear.' I was chuckling most of the way through" (Gene Simmons PR). This original recording would be tightened up for release on Gene Simmons' 2004 "Asshole" album.

100. If I Had a Gun

(3:19) - Alex Chuaqui
Recorded: 2002
Source:
Studio: Bag's Living Room, Vancouver, BC, Canada

Originally credited to both Bag and Gene on the "Asshole" album, the song reverts solely to Bag's credit on the Vault. According to Gene, "Bag, who's the first new artist on Simmons Records, wrote that. I reshaped the song a bit and also added the bridge. I was struck by the poignancy of 'look at me with my makeup messed, I'm so ugly, I've never been kissed.' We all feel that way, sometimes" (Gene Simmons PR). In the Vault liner notes, Gene goes into a bit more detail about the depression perspective of the subject matter. Like the other songs involving Bag, this would be recorded in Bag's living room and features Bag on all instruments. This recording appears to be the same source material, albeit in rearranged form, as the original album version.

101. I Walk Alone

(3:26) - Gene Simmons / Bruce Kulick
Recorded: 199?
Source:
Studio:
The original Gene vocal demo of the song Bruce would ultimately sing on the "Carnival of Souls" album. Not surprisingly, there are substantial differences in the vocal delivery and the song has a different character overall.

102. Seduction of the Innocent

(5:06) - Gene Simmons / Scott Van Zen
Recorded: 199?
Source:
Studio:
According to Gene, the melody of this song is the oldest melody reference point contained on the Vault. The C-G melody formed one of his very first songs, "My Girl Bought Me Chocolate Ice Cream," which had an unsurprisingly Middle Eastern sound. Fast forward decades and this would become one of the first song titles mentioned by Gene that was being worked on for the follow-up to "Revenge." Co-written with Scott Van Zen, the demo provides a striking contrast (like all the COS demos) to the album version.

103. Lonely Is the Hunter

(3:01) - Gene Simmons
Recorded: 1983
Source:

Studio:
Inspired by Humble Pie, Gene makes it clear in the Vault liner notes that he prefers this slimy demo to the version produced on the "Animalize" album. He also admits to not being present when the track was recorded for that KISS album.

104. Never Gonna Leave You #1
(2:21) - Gene Simmons
Recorded: 1977
Source: 4-track
Studio: Apartment closet
Gene suggests that this song was one of the first he wrote after obtaining his Tascam 4-track recorder. Inspired by the sort of chorus many Motown songs had.

105. I Ain't Comin' Back
(2:57) - Gene Simmons
Recorded: 197?
Source: 4-track
Studio: Apartment closet
A bass heavy Motown inspired dance track. Gene performs all the instrumentation, and a little Roland amp adds character. If the "Vault" has shockers, this may well be one to draw listener's attentions to. This is the same song as disk 10 track 9 (meaning there are only 165 songs on the Vault).

106. Never Gonna Leave You #2
(3:16) - Gene Simmons
Recorded: 199?
Source: 16-track
Studio:
An attempt, with Eric Singer and Bruce Kulick, to update the sound of the original demo. From the improved recording environment, it certainly sounds far better while losing all the essence of the original.

Disk 08

Running time: 45:55

107. We Rocked It All Night

(3:23) - Gene Simmons
Recorded: 2009
Source:
Studio:
Gene's semi-autobiographical ode to many of the things and places that are, and have been, important parts of his life — almost a new riff on "Rockin' in the U.S.A." Written for "Sonic Boom," it recycled the "All the Kids in Painted Faces" and "you drive us wild, we'll drive you crazy" lyrics. It likely includes Tommy and Eric.

108. She's Rotten to the Core

(3:32) - Gene Simmons / Bruce Kulick
Recorded: Early 1990s
Source:
Studio:
A riff that refused to die and one that is illustrative of Gene's writing mantra of never abandoning an idea. While there is an exquisite demo of "Rotten to the Core," dating back to 1976 when Gene initially demoed the idea with Starz drummer Joe X, this song is a different beast. Written with Bruce Kulick the song is a different song with different lyrics being utilized, and Bruce breathing fresh life into the riff and structure. A version of this song, with Lita Ford on lead vocals, was released on her "Time Capsule" archival album in April 2016. It included Gene on bass, Bruce on guitars, and Roger Carter on drums.

109. S&M Love

(2:370) - Gene Simmons
Recorded: 2002
Source:
Studio:

Gene and Tommy attempting to update the ancient "Sweet & Dirty Love," given a different title to differentiate it from the other versions on the Vault.

110. Sweet & Dirty Love

(3:19) - Gene Simmons
Recorded: 2003
Source:
Studio:
Another version of the song with Tommy (and Eric Singer) with it approaching the form that would be used on Gene's "Asshole" album in 2004. Compared with that version, the bass is not as overbearing in the mix nor is the mastering as brick-walled; which will make this Vault versions superior for some listener's ears. Gene suggests that he wrote this song "years" before Queen's "Tie Your Mother Down," though with that classic being recorded in the second half of 1976 it's a pointless exercise to one-up a clear winner.

111. Jelly Roll
(1:52) - Gene Simmons
Recorded: 1975/6
Source: Acetate
Studio:

This transfer may have come from the same 12" acetate that was sold in the 2000 Butterfields KISS auction — all of the static fingerprints from that vinyl transfer are present. The riff grew out of Gene playing with the "Nothin' to Lose" riff in a different key.

112. Just Gimme Love #2
(3:44) - Gene Simmons
Recorded: 1997
Source:
Studio:

Another attempt in developing the song, that would ultimately become "You Wanted the Best," with Tommy Thayer on guitar. Gene suggests this was worked on the same day "Say You Don't Want It" was recorded. Many of the core lyrics of YWTB are present, even if there is a completely different chorus (as referenced by the title). It's pretty clear that it's from early in the "Psycho Circus" album cycle.

113. You Wanted the Best
(3:36) - Gene Simmons
Recorded: 1997
Source:
Studio:

With the song approaching its final form, Gene demoed it with Tommy on guitar singing all the vocals himself. Where he planned the other members to sing, he shouts out their names as placeholders. Lyrics are not complete, so there is some scatting in sections. With an increased tempo and harsher sound than the album version, the demo provides an interesting contrast.

114. Just Gimme Love #1

(3:25) - Gene Simmons
Recorded: 1977
Source:
Studio:

Gene suggests that this demo was recorded while the band were on tour at some small-town studio. He plays all the instruments, though there is a click-track in place of drums and backing vocals are by random people hanging around the studio. "Love Is Blind" apparently dates from the same day.

115. Hit the Ground

(2:07) - Gene Simmons
Recorded: 200?
Source:
Studio:

Inspired by "Shake Your Moneymaker," the demo of "Hit the Ground (Put Your Money Where Your Mouth Is)" was recorded with Tommy and Eric. This recording is the initial sketch of the idea, so there are no lyrics for the song yet

116. Who Said So

(1:53) - Gene Simmons
Recorded: 2011
Source:
Studio: Conway Recording Studios Studio C, Hollywood, CA

Gene suggests that this song was recorded on the same day as "Are You Real" and "Guilty Pleasures" with Eric and Tommy. With no lyrics, the inspiration of Pete Townshend is clear, and it's more of a hopeful jam that illustrates the creative process. Gene working on this song with Tommy and Eric was featured in studio footage posted on YouTube April 20, 2011.

117. Bad Bad Lovin'

(3:12) - Gene Simmons
Recorded: 1978
Source: 24-track

Studio:
This demo is the version of the song that developed after "Calling Dr. Love" split into a separate song. With wolf-whistles, saxophone, and female backing vocals it's the version that has circulated in fan circles for decades. However, two repetitions of the chorus are omitted at the end (one with the "you're a brazen hussy" and the other with the "so fine" spoken sections). More importantly, the full introduction of the song is present — something that had been missing on many circulating copies. The quality is also excellent.

118. I'm Paralyzed
(3:31) - Gene Simmons / Bob Ezrin
Recorded: 1988/9
Source:
Studio: Fortress Studios, Los Angeles, CA
This song was written by Gene and Bob and just missed being included on the "Hot in the Shade" album. Additional work would be done on the song for its inclusion on the "Revenge" album in 1991/2.

119. Chrome Heart
(3:33) - Gene Simmons / Bruce Kulick
Recorded: 1986
Source:
Studio:
In the Vault book, a picture of the original handwritten lyrics to the song are included and clearly note "Simmons/Rice." Rice, as in Howard Rice, the co-writer of several 1983 songs with Gene — notably "Any Way You Slice It." However, this demo is co-credited to Bruce Kulick and recycles the title utilizing a riff that Bruce had brought to Gene. This was a demo purportedly presented to Ron Nevison for the "Crazy Nights" album and is particularly lo-fidelity, but it again begs the question what that album could have been...

120. 'Til the End of Time

(3:11) - Gene Simmons
Recorded: 1993/4?
Source:
Studio:

Chock full of discordant sounds, the lack of details in the Vault book force one to try and catalog this song and it would seem to fit in the "Carnival of Souls" era with the similarities with sections of "Seduction of the Innocent." Since Gene will happily reinterpret riffs and ideas already on KISS albums, it's impossible to know (at this point) whether it was before or after 1997, though it certainly reuses the "Legends Never Die" chorus.

121. Thou Shalt Not

(3:00) - Gene Simmons / Jesse Damon
Recorded: 1991
Source:
Studio:

This instrumental track is a different version (or take) than that which previously circulated and is of stunning quality. There appears to be a guide vocal very low in the mix.

Disk 09
Running time: 53:30

122. It's Gonna Be Alright
(4:29) - Gene Simmons / Mikel Japp
Recorded: 1982
Source:
Studio: Mikel Japp's Kitchen

This song was among five Gene offered to the Glaswegian band Heavy Pettin', who had opened for KISS on the European leg of the "Lick It Up" tour (along with Helix), in 1984. Ultimately, Smashed Gladys eventually recorded a version of the song titled "Give It All You Got" on their Gene involved 1985 demo prior to being signed by a record label. A demo tape he circulated including it was dated Sept. 24, 1983.

Fans may be disappointed that the version included on the Vault is not vastly superior to the best copies that have circulated for decades. However, they should be reminded that the recording methodology was likely a limiting factor. Mitch Weissman, who demoed the song with Gene recalled, the "demo is Gene over the click track. Mikel Japp had this riff, I did the passing chords, they were kind of Beatle-esque." Mikel had only met Gene for the first time, at SIR Studios while the band was rehearsing material for "KISS Killers." He and Gene would write at Diana Ross' house, where Gene was staying at the time.

123. It's Gonna Be Alright #2
(3:14) - Gene Simmons / Mikel Japp
Recorded: 198?
Source:
Studio:

Like many other demos, this effort (with Bruce Kulick on guitar) was an attempt to update the song and knock it into usable form with additional instrumentation.

124. Everybody Knows #1 ✪
(3:54) - Gene Simmons
Recorded: 198?
Source:
Studio:

This song was originally released in 2003 on Gene Simmons' "Sex Money KISS" audio lunchbox bonus disk and on the Japanese version of "Asshole." Identical through first 45 seconds, then arrangement and lyrics change. The sound quality is substantially improved on the Vault versus the 2003 version. Deliberately mimicking Ace's intro to "Rock Bottom," with a 12-string guitar, is one Tommy Thayer.

125. Everybody Knows #2
(3:43) - Gene Simmons
Recorded:
Source:
Studio:

Losing the retro guitar in favor of something grungier, Gene turns the song into a completely different creature with a different arrangement and vocal delivery.

126. You're all That I Want ✪
(4:05) - Gene Simmons
Recorded: 1977
Source:
Studio:
Previously released on the 2001 KISS Box — though from a different master excluding the count-in — this recording features a slight arrangement change. With Paul Stanley on backing vocals, the two had demoed the song while on tour. The song appears on a compilation of Gene's demo ideas dated 1979, though he has also previously stated that the song was written in 1977.

127. Kids with Painted Faces
(3:11) - Darren Leader / Gene Simmons
Recorded: 2002
Source:
Studio:
Recycling elements of "I Am Yours" and a lyric from "Master of Flash" this was the second of two songs Gene demoed with Steel Panther's Darren Leader (who also co-wrote "I Wait" which also appears on the Vault) in April/May 2002.

128. I Wanna Rule the World
(5:00) - Gene Simmons
Recorded: 1997?
Source:
Studio:
During the chaotic "Psycho Circus" sessions nearly 20 songs were recorded for use for the album. This Gene Simmons composition was written with Ace Frehley in mind. It was, however, not used, even with a great "Here's hoping all your dreams come true, forever" lyric which ties in nicely with Gene's other material on the album. According to Gene, the song "was very Mott the Hoople, crossed with a

bombastic John Bonham beat. You British like the heavier stuff, but we purposely left out a lot of the heavier ones because the record as it stands makes a much stronger musical statement"(Classic Rock, 1/99). The version on the Vault differs from the recently leaked "Psycho Circus" material in that it is clearly a different recording, which may be a sonic victim to multiple tape bounces.

129. Rule the World #2
(4:04) - Gene Simmons / Scott Van Zen
Recorded: 1993/4
Source:
Studio:
According to Gene, this is a completely different song to the one that precedes it and chronologically was written after that original idea. It was simply a matter of using a similar title. Heavy and grungy, it would have fit during the "Carnival of Souls" era. The recording likely dates from 1993/4 because it features a small musical section that ended up in the final arrangement of "I Walk Alone."

130. Damn, I'm Good
(3:25) - Gene Simmons
Recorded: 1993/4?
Source:
Studio:
From the school of "Sticky Goo," Demon in full-flight fun jamming with Eric Singer on drums: "Raise your hands to stars above, pay a friendly visit with your Dr. Love // Damn, I'm good." With odd chords the R&B meets CCR infused song provides yet another side of the demon.

131. Dial L for Love
(3:35) - Gene Simmons / Adam Mitchell / Eric Carr
Recorded: 1987
Source:
Studio:
It had previously been thought that this song had never been fully recorded during the "Crazy Nights" era, so the

inclusion of a pristine studio vocal (by Gene) was a surprise on the Vault. Eric had commented that the song was not good enough — at that point — to make it onto the album, and that it was felt that it was a work in progress. As the primary writer, Eric had taken the song to Gene and Adam for polishing, something which he had done several times. Gene has commented: "Eric and I co-wrote a song called 'Dial L for Love,' a real fine tune. If it won't be on a KISS record it'll be on somebody's record" (Rock Scene Spotlights #2). A rough demo, which did not include any completed vocals, was finally released in 2011 on Eric's "Unfinished Business" album. At the time, it was erroneously assumed to be the best there was, but good enough for fans to get some idea about what the song sounded like.

132. Just Like the Movies #1
(2:44) - Gene Simmons / Stephen Bishop
Recorded: 1979/80
Source:
Studio:
After meeting solo artist Stephen Bishop, via Cher, the two decided to try and write a song together. Gene recounted the song-writing session, "We were just talking, rambling... and he [Stephen Bishop] said 'just like the movies, I feel like Romeo.' I go 'that's a song!'... The melody came very fast once I heard that" (Rhino PR). Gene took Stephen's original chord idea and title and completed the song. Using Latin beat drumdrops, the resulting demo has an odd semi-disco/easy listening vibe. The song shares a break section that is very similar musically to the one used on KISS' "She's so European" in 1980... Gene and Stephen would remain friends for several years, even getting turned down trying to access a backstage party following a Billy Joel concert and sharing a dinner with Ted Nugent.

133. I Know Who You Are ✪
(3:22) - Gene Simmons
Recorded:

Source:
Studio:
The basic chords and melody of this demo later became "Living in Sin" on Gene's 1978 solo album. Like, "Reputation," which is another variant and was previously released on the 2014 "KISS 40" package (and detailed in those liner notes as a leftover from the "Love Gun" sessions), the song is illustrative of the process many Gene songs take to reach final fruitarian. Joe X from Starz plays the drums on the recording with Gene handling the rest of the instrumentation himself.

134. Sweet Temptation

(2:45) - Gene Simmons
Recorded: 1979/80
Source:
Studio:
Verse and break melody elements of this demo would be recycled by Bob Ezrin for the "Elder" version of "Only You." All instruments by Gene, with the addition of a drum machine.

135. Are You Always This Hot

(2:55) - Gene Simmons / Adam Mitchell
Recorded: 1987
Source:
Studio:
The semi-legendary 12th song recorded for the "Crazy Nights," which recycled a title originally used by Adam Mitchell for a solo composition used in the "World According to Garp" theatrical movie release in 1982. By the time he was working on material for the 1987 album, Gene decided that he liked Adam's title and suggested that the two write a new song using it. Strangely, considering the quality of the guitar playing, Bruce Kulick was never a fan of the song, regardless of how deep in the process it went for the album.

136. Fourever
(3:04) - Gene Simmons
Recorded: 1978
Source: 24-track
Studio:

This song was recorded around the same time as "Bad Bad Lovin'," and like it comes from source material that is substantially improved from the version that has circulated for collectors for decades. It also features saxophone and female backing vocals. Unlike the circulating demo a 10 second drum intro has been removed as have roughly 20 seconds of the ending repetition of the chorus.

Disk 10

Running time: 42:31

137. Take It Like A Man #2

(2:43) - Gene Simmons
Recorded: 1997
Source:
Studio:

This lower form demo was an attempt to reinterpret the original demo and update it for use on the "Psycho Circus" album with separate verse sections for each of the band members. Where musically it is similar to the older version, it is very much incomplete lyrically and Gene instead injects humorous callouts for each of his erstwhile band members. With Bruce and Eric participating musically the musical level is definitely taken up from the original and the piece is heavier.

138. Take It Like A Man #1

(2:35) - Gene Simmons
Recorded: 1983
Source:
Studio:

These first two tracks are flipped on the CD versus their order listed in the accompanying "Vault" book. Recoded on his trusted 4-track this lo-fi demo has circulated for decades, but the improvement in source quality is notable. Often lumped in with the so-called "Asylum" demos, it more than likely dates from earlier than 1985. That tape itself may possibly have been a collection of Gene songs that he was simply offering to other acts and covering a spectrum of years — just ideas in search of a writing credit on someone's released product.

139. Have Mercy, Baby

(3:44) - Gene Simmons / Bruce Kulick
Recorded: November 1986
Source: 4-track > 24-track

Studio:

Once assumed to have never made it past the song-writing stage, this demo clearly proves otherwise. If submitted for the "Crazy Nights" album, it's clear that Gene's material wasn't as weak during that era as has been suggested for the period, but that his focus and commitment was likely more the reason his material wasn't making KISS albums.

140. We Won't Take It Anymore

(2:59) - Gene Simmons / Eric Carr
Recorded: Summer, 1983
Source: 4-track
Studio: Hotel Room, New York City

Recorded in a hotel room during the recording of the "Lick it Up" album. This song was offered to Scottish rockers Heavy Pettin' while Gene was on location filming "Runaway" and included on a demo tape dated 9/14/83. Having circulated for decades, the demo is one of the more complete musical ideas from the so-called "Asylum" demos and provides additional evidence of the musical ideas and positive contributions Eric Carr was bringing to the band. Eric plays guitar on the track.

141. My Babe

(1:43 - Gene Simmons / Eric Carr
Recorded: Summer, 1983
Source: 4-track
Studio: Hotel Room, New York City

Based on chord pattern Eric brought to Gene to which he added the melody and lyric. Recorded in a hotel room during the recording of the "Lick It Up." Another song without purpose in search of something more.

142. Eat Your Heart Out

(2:31) - Gene Simmons
Recorded: 1977/8
Source:
Studio: Electric Lady Studios, New York City

Recorded with Joe X from Starz on drums. With full 70's feel, this demo was the precursor to a song with the same title that would finally find a home on a KISS studio album in 2012 (though Gene had also written a version in the mid-1980s with Mitch Weissman). The suspended chords in the music are reference to the catchy songs Gene would hear on the radio, by bands like the Doobie Brothers, at the time. Roughly 20 seconds of repetition are removed at the end of the song to shorten it slightly.

143. Nine Lives
(3:25) - Gene Simmons / Davitt Sigerson
Recorded: 1986
Source: 4-track
Studio:
Co-written with Mercury's Vice President at the apartment Gene shared with Shannon Tweed. With a slinky melodic feel akin to watching a cat walk around; the song ponders a cat's nine lives. Recorded on 4-track with later lead overdubs by Bruce Kulick.

144. Howling for Your Love
(2:16) - Gene Simmons
Recorded: 1976
Source:
Studio:
Long circulating, this demo brings many of the players Gene would use in the mid-1970s, to record his ideas, together. Not only are the girls from the Group with No Name featured on backing vocals, the inimitable Binky Philips, then formerly of the Planets, is on lead guitar. In terms of lyrics, it's Gene writing for his character.

145. I Ain't Coming Back
(2:56) - Gene Simmons
An error, this is the same as disk 7, track 14. Oops...

146. Granny Takes a Trip

(2:06) - Gene Simmons
Recorded: 1994
Source:
Studio:

Not enough details are present in the Vault book to determine much about this heavy, albeit brief, idea. Sonically it could easily date from the "Carnival of Souls" era. "Granny Takes a Trip" was a famed fashion boutique in London that led rise to many similar stores, including branches in Los Angeles and New York. As a title, the possibilities were endless, and Gene certainly isn't singing about fashion.

147. Piece of the Rock

(3:44) - Gene Simmons / Robert Fleischman
Recorded: 2000s
Source:
Studio:

An unusual collaboration with ex-Journey and ex-Vinnie Vincent Invasion vocalist Robert Fleischman, though Gene handles the vocal duties with Robert assisting on the chorus. Robert had brought Gene a few ideas and this piece was one that resonated with Gene, which he changed into a form he liked. Robert provided the instrumentation. This low fidelity recording embodies the term, "demo," meaning a demonstration of a musical idea that can serve as a blueprint for further development (or not to forget what you were thinking musically at the time).

148. Rock It

(2:22) - Gene Simmons
Recorded: 198?
Source:
Studio:

Gene dates this track to the 1980s, having been inspired by English bands like the Fine Young Cannibals who were blending multiple genres and opening new musical doors as a result. Although the drums cop the feel of the Fine Young Cannibals" #1 hit "She Drives Me Crazy," the melody and overall feel of the song is closer to "So Alive," a 1989 #3 hit by British band Love & Rockets, another 80's new-wave/dance-pop style band.

149. Sticky Goo

(2:59) - Gene Simmons
Recorded: 1993/4?
Source:
Studio:

Mr. Frehley has "Funk Rock" in his deep catalog of unreleased material. Gene's Bo Diddley beat based "Sticky Goo," is the sort of material that always appears when a musician is just playing and searching for ideas. Sometimes, when jamming, a seemingly stupid idea emerges, that just captures the musician's attention for a while. It may not be serious, but it is a fun interlude and possibly entertaining. And where it may lead, often nowhere, but who knows. Musically, it's ahead of the game, lyrically, desperately seeking something.

150. Love Came to Me

(3:25) - Gene Simmons
Recorded: 197?
Source:
Studio:

Dating from 1977, possibly even earlier, "Love Came to Me" was a development piece that, when demoed, featured Gene on all the instruments and higher-key backing vocals. It was inspired by the disco/dance-rock material that was being performed by other artists such as Rod Stewart, earlier than Paul was inspired to write "I Was Made for Lovin' You." While this demo has circulated for decades the clear version included hear is a nice improvement that brings many new musical details to the surface. Gene suggests the song was pitched to KISS in 1979 but was rejected.

151. Roar of the Greasepaint

(3:03) - Gene Simmons
Recorded: 199?
Source:
Studio:

The demo precursor to "Journey of 1,000 Years," many of the elements of the "Psycho Circus" song are present, as are Tommy Thayer and Eric Singer on this recording. The title was based on a 1965 musical, though of course "the roar of the greasepaint, smell of the crowd" appealed to Gene more than the more obvious "smell of the greasepaint, roar of the crowd."

the master cutting room

33 1/3   STEREO

GENE SIMMONS

ROTTON TO THE CORE
DAILY PLANET
BURNING UP WITH FEVER

Bonus Disk

Running time: 38:43

152. Feel Like Heaven

(3:03) - Gene Simmons
Recorded: 1978/9
Source:
Studio:

One step up from the original low fidelity (and slightly vulgar) recorded-in-a-closet demo that had circulated for years, this demo includes Gene, a bass, and a children's synthesizer that he'd later use to transform "War Machine." At the beginning of 1981 KISS recorded a version of this song, at primarily at Ace's home with overdubs being added at Penny Lane Studios in New York City; before that album transformed into the much maligned "Elder" project.

153. Obnoxious

(2:37) - Gene Simmons
Recorded: 1978
Source:
Studio:

According to Gene, this song was written on the road and recorded the same day as "Eat Your Heart Out" and "Love Is Blind." The chorus was later recycled later as the more familiar "Reputation." This version of the demo had circulated for many years using that more familiar title, though the Vault features a speed-corrected version that omits the instrumental introduction — essentially the verse music that would otherwise would have resulted in a track duration of 2:53.

154. Mina-San, Mina-San

(2:29) - Gene Simmons
Recorded: 2013
Source:
Studio:

Offered to Japanese girl band Momoiro Clover Z, this song was ultimately ignored in favor of "Samurai Son." The title translates as "Everybody, everybody," and the song recycles some of the musical elements from the "Fourever" demo.

155. I Have Just Begun to Fight
(3:24) - Gene Simmons
Recorded: 1978
Source:
Studio:
While this blatant attempt to recycle the chords of "Calling Dr. Love" is often described as being an "Asylum" demo, it was originally demoed in late 1978/early 1979. The demo circulated in shortened form, for decades, prior to a substantial upgrade surfacing in the early 2000s. At the time, Gene Simmons was working with the boy-band Virgin (who were also conveniently managed by Bill Aucoin). He produced studio recordings for an album that was never completed or released. At the same time Gene was recording demo material with Virgin drummer Chuck Billings. Chuck, and Virgin's guitarist, Tom Moody, were also present at the KISS Magic Mountain, Valencia show for "KISS Meets the Phantom of the Park." 4 or 5 songs would be recorded, including one, whose title is currently unknown, later being re-recorded for a KISS album. The Vault version does cut one repetition of the song's riff from the beginning reducing its duration by four seconds.

156. It's Funny, But It Ain't No Joke
(2:33) - Gene Simmons
Recorded: 1978/9
Source: 4-track
Studio: Home studio, New York City
Dating from after "Love by Invitation," Gene recycled the verse of that song and added a new chorus.

157. Love by Invitation
(3:18) - Gene Simmons

Recorded: 1978
Source:
Studio: Los Angeles, CA
Gene dates this oddity from around the same time as "Fourever."

158. Dorothy Lamour
(2:43) - Gene Simmons
Recorded: 1980
Source:
Studio:
Dorothy was actress and singer best remembered for appearing in the "Road to..." series (1940–52) of comedies starring Bing Crosby and Bob Hope. Her name, and an afternoon watching television, was enough to inspire Gene to write this song. The demo was recorded with members of the Aucoin managed band Spider (Anton Fig and Holly Knight) providing the backing instrumentation.

Amusingly, when Gene and Paul made a guest appearance on the Fox network cartoon, "Family Guy," in 2002, their episode, "Road to Europe," was a parody of the movie series. During the episode Peter and Lois attend a KISS concert with Lois not realizing that she had once dated Chaim before he became Gene.

159. Queen of Hearts
(3:11) - Peppy Castro / Gene Simmons
Recorded: 1980
Source:
Studio:
Dating from around the time "Naked City" was written, Gene took an original demo written by Peppy Castro and added the melody and lyrics. This demo includes Peppy on keyboards and guitar, along with a drum machine and synthesizer on which Gene added his vocal and backgrounds.

160. My Lorraine

(1:57) - Gene Simmons
Recorded: 1980
Source: Boom Box
Studio: Kitchen

Another of Gene's ancient demos; likely dating from 1966, which he would later simply record in his kitchen as an exercise in trying to remember the song. He also revisited the piece on his "Gene Simmons Family Jewels" TV show.

161. Leeta ✪

(2:23) - Gene Simmons
Recorded: 1969/70
Source: Acetate
Studio: Sanders Recording Studio, Brooklyn, NY

"Leeta" demonstrates Gene's musical roots, more than being a snapshot of where he was at musically in 1969/70, though this is another of the earliest songs Gene wrote and is heavy on the harmonies that had made his idols, The Beatles, famous. There are multiple sources available for this recording, certainly 2 different acetates and Gene's 1970 publishing reel. In his 2003 "Sex, Money, KISS" book Gene recollected that the song was the second one he'd written...

This transfer is not the same as the 2001 KISS "Box Set" transfer. In fact, it sounds identical to a 2000 transfer of the B-side of the 10" "Stanley the Parrot" acetate including the original excessive digital processing of transfer, right down to the acetate snaps, crackles, and pops. As for what happened to the 7" Sanders acetate, that's currently unknown, but like the 10" acetate it may have ended up unnoted in someone's auction lot... Like "Stanley the Parrot," the musicians on the track were members of Gene's college band, Bullfrog Bheer, with possible later overdubs by Brooke Ostrander.

162. Put on Your Slippers

(2:24) - Gene Simmons
Recorded: 1970
Source: 2-track reel
Studio: Brooke's Nutley, NJ Living Room

Likely another of the tracks recorded with Brooke Ostrander on keys for use on Gene's 12 song demo reel. The original submission letter that accompanied the reel noted that the song's length was 2:40.

163. Gypsy Nights

(2:52) - Gene Simmons
Recorded: 1978/9
Source:
Studio:

Dating from the same period as "Feel like Heaven" when Gene was feeling inspired by ELO.

164. Eskimo Sun

(3:08) - Gene Simmons
Recorded: 1970

Source: 2-track reel
Studio:
A song performed live by the precursor to Wicked Lester, Rainbow, a recording of this song was included on Gene's 12 song 7" demo reel in 1970. The song is notable for being the source of the melody of "Only You," inspired by The Beatles' "Because," which Gene had started to write in the late 1970s and was ultimately recorded for "The Elder." Originally titled "Eskimo Sun (A Six Month Waltz)."

165. A Reevus in the Eye — Nancy

(1:25) - Gene Simmons
Recorded: 1969/70
Source: 2-track reel
Studio: South Fallsburg, NY / Brooke's Nutley, NJ Living Room
Initially recorded solo by Gene in upstate New York and later overdubbed with Brooke's keyboards, this song was included on Gene's 12 song 7" demo reel. The original title for this demo was "A Reevus in the Eye — Nancy," with "reevus" making as much sense as Steve Miller's "the pompatous of love" in English...

166. My Uncle Is a Raft

(1:16) - Gene Simmons
Recorded: 1966
Source: 2-track
Studio: Larry Martinelli's Brooklyn Basement
Fans first heard a taste of this ancient song, which is one of the very earliest Gene wrote, when he performed part of this song with an acoustic guitar during an episode of his Family Jewels television show. This song has become the primary song & story Gene tells during the Vault experience due to its connection to the beginning of Gene's musical career and inspiration, when he was just learning how to play chords on the guitar. The song was recorded with Gene's school friends, Mark Nyberg and Larry Martinelli.

The Vault Experiences

(Various dates have been scheduled / rescheduled — at time of printing)

September 15, 2017 - Electric Lady Studios, New York City, NY

Notes:

- The first Producer Experience was conducted in the Studio A control room at the legendary Electric Lady Studios. Footage from the event was used in various online promotions.

October 1 - Luminous Sound Studios, Dallas, TX

Notes:

-This Producer Experience took place in the control room of Studio A at this recording facility.

- While numerous Producer experiences were scheduled, these two were apparently the only ones that took place.

December 31 - EBay "Home" Experience **CANCELLED

Notes:

- Initially, a New Year's Eve "Vault Home Experience: EBay Auction" was planned, but never got past the point of scheduling.

January 6, 2018 - Capitol Studios, Los Angeles, CA

Special guest(s): Ace Frehley, Bruce Kulick, Eric Singer

Notes:

- The first Vault Experience was hosted in Studio A at the legendary Capitol Studios. Film crews were on hand to capture footage and interview fans for commercials for the Vault.

- Gene walked the awaiting fan line, who'd been plied with Moneybags sodas while they waited in the California sun, bumping fists and delivering one-liners.

- "Vault" book author Ken Sharp was also present.

- Following Ace's arrival the two took to the stage for a clearly impromptu banter session that lasted nearly 30 minutes. Gene later returned to the stage for his separate 30-minute songs & stories session concluding with Eric Singer, Ace, and Bruce Kulick joining him on stage for an additional 15 minutes.

(It's a side-table! It's a chair! It's a drum!)

January 20 - John Varvatos, Detroit, MI
January 21 - John Varvatos, Detroit, MI
Special guest(s): None.
Notes:
- Gene told local press, "Everybody thinks of us as a New York band but, truly, it was Detroit that opened up their arms for us. When we were playing thousand seaters in the rest of the country, we actually sold out three days at Cobo... For me, this is the second vault event anywhere in America. For me it's homecoming... I've got to do this for me; this is my bucket list. Before this journey is over, I want to meet the fans who made my life possible" (Detroit WJBK, 1/22/2018).

(Reunited. Ace & Gene. Photo: Nigel Dreiner — used with permission)

January 27 - Walt Grace Vintage, Miami, FL

Special guest(s): Ace Frehley, Maria Contessa

Notes:

- From a local review: "Like a divorced couple sharing old stories of their high-profile marriage, the duo kept an audience — which included Barry Gibb's musician son Stephen Gibb — rapt during a freewheeling Q&A session that touched on their time together in KISS. The pair, sitting in front of a wall of guitars that collector Frehley coveted, also strummed acoustic guitars. This led Simmons to quip how difficult it was to play a vintage tune like KISS' 'She' unplugged" (Miami Herald, 2/2/2018).

January 28 - Home Vault Experience, Miami, FL

Special guest(s): Ace Frehley

Notes:

- To date, the sole $50,000 "Home" Experience sold. Oddly, Vanilla Ice was in attendance.

February 10 - Monster Mini Golf @ Rio, Las Vegas, NV

Special guest(s): Bob Kulick

Notes:
- A second planned "Vault" date on the following day was instead turned into a Gene Simmons Master Class custom bass event.

February 17 - City Winery, Boston, MA
Special guest(s): None.
Notes:
- Gene explained the contents of the Vault in a review of the event: "'You can call it a labor of love, but really these songs have just been up in the attic and I didn't want to let them die,' said Simmons, who was wearing large mirrored shades. 'It's like your children. You want to bring them out in the fresh air and let people see how beautiful they are.' Simmons also took the opportunity to lament online streaming services, and the effect they have on bands. '[Artists] will never get the chance we had because there's no record industry to speak of, and that goes back to the fans who refuse to pay for music,' he said. 'You can say Spotify and Shmotify, but one tenth of one cent for a download is just not going to be able to do it ... As soon as you take something and don't pay the artist, they can't afford to make a living and they die'" (Boston Globe, 2/18/2018).

February 18 - Trocadero, Philadelphia, PA
Special guest(s): None.
Notes:
- From a local review: "Simmons spoke for about an hour, dark shades on inside the nearly pitch-black theatre, cradling a Les Paul tuned to E (his preferred tuning is D, as he made quite lightheartedly yet borderline-hurtfully clear to the long-haired gentleman responsible for pre-tuning his guitars), breaking down and explaining his approach to songwriting in far greater detail than I ever would have anticipated. Citing a song called 'Smile' written by silent movie era star Charlie Chaplin as his personal favorite,

Simmons explained his thoughts on songwriting by half-singing the first few lines. 'Smile, though your heart is aching / Smile, though your heart is breaking,' Simmons crooned as a transfixed crowd listened. 'That's a perfect song. Because the name of the song is 'Smile.' The very first lyric you hear is 'smile'. It ends with the word 'smile.'" He goes on to compare this song against 'Sunshine of Your Love' by Cream, noodling his way through the long-winded riffs and meandering lyrics. 'It takes two minutes to get into the chorus,' says Simmons.

It was at this point I realized I didn't know who this man was. What I expected from this event and from this man was the image I (and probably many others) have cobbled together from half-heard anecdotes and way-too-easy punchlines. I expected 'The Demon' and found only Mr. Simmons. I expected a sales pitch and found only perfectly genuine and completely original insight into the mechanics of songwriting. In fact, even Simmons simply citing Charlie Chaplain as one of his favorite songwriters of all time will remain as one of the most mind-blowing and unanticipated things I've ever heard" (Jersey Man Magazine).

February 24 - Music Record Shop 303, St. Louis, MO
Special guest(s): Ace Frehley
Notes:
- From a local review: "The good times started at the front door, where the friendliest staff you've ever met welcomed all 120 guests inside one by one, making each person feel special. They also happily answered every little question, keeping the energy high and the people excited. These kind of long events can easily slip into tedium, but the staff was not about to let that happen. Upon arrival, guests were asked to sign a photo release form and were given what looked like a tour laminate. Then they all hung out together in the lobby, speaking enthusiastically about their love for Simmons and about KISS Kruises and other fan events that

they've attended. (Did you know the KISS Kruise has a waiting list?) It was here, at the very beginning, that it became clear who had shown up for the event. Yep, it was the KISS Army. And they were in full uniform. They looked amazing in all of their gear, showing it off to each other and having a great time" (Riverfront Times, 2/26/2018).

March 17 - John Varvatos, Mayfair, London, England
Special guest(s): None.

March 18 - Frankfurt, Germany **POSTPONED
Notes:
- This sold-out "Vault" experience was cancelled at the last moment due to health issues affecting Gene while he was in London. The date had been rescheduled for two days, July 24–25, by the end of the month

(Screen grab: Peter and Gene reunited, briefly)

March 24 - V.K. Nagrani, New York City, NY
Special guest(s): Peter Criss
Notes:
- Peter Criss stopped by briefly to say "Hi" to Gene. He addressed the crowd thanking them for their support.

March 25 - V.K. Nagrani, New York City, NY
Special guest(s): None.

April 14 - InDo, Nashville, TN
Special guest(s): Vinnie Vincent, the Gene Simmons Band
Notes:
- Added to the schedule in early Dec.
- Vinnie arrived a bit late for the event, due to travel challenges with a storm, resulting in an abbreviated stage session with Gene. Unfortunately, guitar issues again affected the stories session, though it did allow Gene time to strum through "Every Breath You Take" and "Take It Easy," as an illustration of what can be done with the basics. Gene then illustrated how "I Love It Loud" evolved out of the Who's "My Generation." Most importantly, Gene recalled how the lift section of "I Love It Loud" was written to be included in one of Paul's "Killers" songs, but that Paul had rejected it. That provided Gene the inspiration to turn it into a song on its own. Musically limited, part of "Not for the Innocent" was teased, with Gene remembering the main riff of the song. After just 20 minutes together, Gene had to return to his Vault presentation duties. Vinnie remained on stage for another 20 minutes and interacted with the audience and bashed through an impromptu acoustic version of "I Love It Loud," relying on the audience for the lyrics/vocals. Vinnie was later presented with a Vault of his own.
- From a local review: "Mr. Simmons arrived at InDo around 11 a.m., greeting fans as he made his way to the stage. He did a short sound check as he chatted with the crowd before taking time to meet briefly with local media then back to his fans. Armed with an acoustic guitar Gene talked about starting KISS 45 years ago and discussed some of the artists who influenced him such as James Brown. Like many seeing the Beatles on The Ed Sullivan show in the 60's was a pivotal moment. For aspiring musicians, he taught the three major chords which are the baseline for a bevy of popular songs.

During his talk and tutorial Gene circled back to 'Wild Thing' a number of times to nail down his point.

(Screen grab: Reunited. Vinnie Vincent & Gene)

Gene thanked Rhino Records for understanding his vision and desire for the 'wow' factor which was his goal for the Vault. He also expressed his appreciation to his supporters who have made his musical aspirations a reality. At times he was emotional when he talked about the dream life he loves so much while openly acknowledging the fans who made it possible. He was also humorous and gracious as he remained in salesman mode to remind those in attendance that there's still time to buy the Vault Experience" (musiccitynashville.org, 4/14/18).
- Jeremy Asbrock, Phil Shouse, and Brent Fitz from Gene Simmons' solo band performed a brief acoustic set with ET Brown filling in on bass until Ryan Cook arrived: Parasite, She, Comin' Home, Let Me Know, See You Tonite, Hard Luck Woman, Hooligan, See You in Your Dreams, Got To Choose, Beth, and 2,000 Man.

April 21 - Private Residence, Dallas, TX
Special guest(s): None.
Notes:

- This experience took place at one of the Vault's Executive Producer's home. As such it was NOT a Home Experience with the family simply making their residence available for Gene's event.

April 28 - Rock & Roll Hall of Fame, Cleveland, OH
Special guest(s): None.
Notes:
- Added to the schedule in early Dec. One fan suffered a stroke while waiting in line for the event and Gene insisted that he get into a mobile stroke unit and receive emergency treatment. Gene would have breakfast with the fan in Oct. to make good on his Vault Experience.

May 6 - Revolution Recording Studios, Toronto, ON, Canada
Special guest(s): None.

May 12 - Chicago Theatre Works, Chicago, IL
Special guest(s): Shannon Tweed
Notes:
- The May 13 date was combined with the previous day.
- Gene was presented with an award from the Shriners for his charitable support of the Shriners Hospitals for Children.

May 26 - Monster Mini Golf @ Rio, Las Vegas, NV
Special guest(s): Paul Stanley, Bob Kulick, Robert Fleischman, the Gene Simmons Band
Notes:
- This second Las Vegas Vault opportunity, again paired with a Gene Simmons Master Class on the following day, was added in early March.
- Paul Stanley arrived at the event some 30 minutes into Gene's Songs & Stories session and the two entertained the audience with good-natured brotherly ribbing and some stories about various songs in the band's catalogue. Song

highlights included part of an early Rainbow/Wicked Lester song and the story of "Detroit Rock City."

- Paul Stanley signed / pre-signed the Vault's being delivered to the lucky purchasers and participated in the presentations of some.

- Gene also spent time with a cancer patient/survivor from St. Jude's Children's Research Hospital (Las Vegas), and a Make-a-Wish recipient.

(Paul: "I wrote 'God of Thunder!'")

June 1 - Gröna Lundsteatern, Stockholm, Sweden

Special guest(s): None.

Notes:

- Gene played part of the ancient, "Movin' On," a Bullfrog Bheer song that was eventually demoed by Wicked Lester, but not recorded, as part of his songs & stories section. He was also able to play part of "Stanley the Parrot," when requested by a fan while not answering the question of why the demo was not on the Vault. He did, however, proceed to play some of "Leeta."

- The day following the event the Gene Simmons Band performed at the legendary Tivoli Gröna Lund (reportedly to an audience of nearly 5,000), during which Gene announced the forthcoming three-year KISS world tour starting in January 2019.

June 3 - Popsenteret, Oslo, Norway
Special guest(s): None.
Notes:
- Added to the schedule in early Dec., this event had sold-out by late-May.

June 9 - Tree Sound Studios, Atlanta, GA
Special guest(s): None.
Notes:
- Rescheduled from the original July 14th date.

June 10 - Midwood Guitar Studio, Charlotte, NC
Special guest(s): None.
Notes:
- Added to the schedule in early Dec.

July 9 - Westin Hotel, Madrid, Spain
Special guest(s): None.
Notes:
- A breakfast Vault Experience with the God of Thunder had been scheduled for the previous day, but the event was instead bumped to the day following KISS' performance at the WiZink Center (formerly the Palacio de Deportes de la Comunidad de Madrid). Additionally, the breakfast component was ultimately scrapped when the event time became afternoon rather than morning. The experience eventually commenced at 4pm...
- No songs & stories performance was conducted at this event.

July 22 - Gibson Brands, Amsterdam Tower, Amsterdam, Holland
Special guest(s): None.
Notes:
- During one Vault experience, Gene grabbed a guitar for a quick musical reminiscence for a KISS-Related-Recordings.com's Jelle Jansen about "Movin' On," a song

he'd written with Anna Dalva during the Bullfrog Bheer era. While not an advertized special guest, Barry Hay (from the band Golden Earring) was at the event...

(Screen grab: Private performance of "Movin' On")

July 24 - Roomers Hotel, Frankfurt, Germany
Special guest(s): Doro Pesch
Notes:
- Rescheduled from the previously postponed March date.

August 29 - Hilton International, Adelaide, SA, Australia
Special guest(s): None.
Notes:
- The same venue was used for the 1995 KISS Convention.
- Ultimately a two-day event with purchasers of the Vault being provided tickets to the Gene Simmons Band / Ace Frehley show at the AEC and the originally scheduled experience being moved to the following day. The usual Gene Simmons band members, though with Accept drummer Christopher Williams subbing for Brent Fitz, backed both Gene and Ace for their sets. Members of the

band, and the singer of Sister Dolls also hung out at the experience.

(Screen grab: Ace & Gene Adelaide Q&A)

- Vault purchasers were welcomed onstage for one song during the show; "Do You Love Me" for the ladies or "I Love It Loud" for the blokes...
- The songs & stories section of the show was replaced with a general Q&A with Gene and Ace, conducted with the pair sitting on the Vaults awaiting delivery to the fans. During the roughly 20-minute session the two amiably fielded all sorts of questions including Vinnie and Paul...
- Vault purchasers were also given access to the show's sound check, which was the first time Ace met Gene's backing band!
- During the event Gene was interviewed by The Project, an Australian current affairs/news talk show that airs on Network Ten. A five-minute segment was broadcast.

August 30 - Festival Hall, West Melbourne, VIC, Australia
Special guest(s): None.

Notes:
- Originally scheduled for the Margaret Court Arena.
- No songs & stories or Q&A session were planned for this event, with the concert also taking place, though Vault purchasers were again given access to the accompanying show sound check. Unfortunately, due to timing little of the sound check would be witnessed.

August 31 - Enmore Theatre, Sydney, NSW, Australia
Special guest(s): None.
Notes:

September 1 - Tivoli Centre, Brisbane, QLD, Australia
Special guest(s): None.
Notes:
- One fan flew in from Mexico for the experience!

October 6–7 - Sweetwater Sound, Ft. Wayne, IN
Special guest(s): None.
Notes:
- A special two-day event, with a $5,000 price tag. Gene was running late for the Q&A session that would start the event — he was having a meal with a fan whose Cleveland Vault experience was interrupted by a stroke!
- During the first recording component, Gene explained concepts such as trademark and dubbing and then laid down the bass track for "Rock and Roll All Nite." Participants were split into small groups to record their chorus vocals for the song. The day concluded with a casual buffet style dinner with Gene chatting and taking photos. He attended the Buddy Guy concert in the evening.
- Day 2 kicked off with Gene's songs and stories following which the Vaults were delivered the participants. Gene joined the Sweetwater Studios house band for a few songs including "Wild Thing," "Cold Gin," and even an attempt at "Crazy Train."

(Screen grab: Gene laying down the bass track for "Rock and Roll All Nite")

November 1 - Spinnaker Lounge, Norwegian Jade, Key West, FL

Special guest(s): None.

Notes:

- Scheduled during the middle of port day during KISS Kruise VIII.

- While Gene didn't conduct a Songs & Stories session, he did participate in a 30-minute Q&A with attending fans.

(Screen grab: Gene with the unsung hero of the "Vault" — Keith!)

December 2 - Monster Mini Golf @ Rio, Las Vegas, NV **CANCELLED

Special guest(s): Tommy Thayer, John 5
Notes:
- Bruce Kulick and his band were also expected to "hang out" at the event...
- This final scheduled "Experience" event was cancelled, due to a "family emergency," on Nov. 29. That emergency resulted in the sad passing of Gene's beloved mother, Flora, on Dec. 6.
- Gene is expected to continue selling Vaults as opportunities warrant during the End of the Road tour in 2019, but the future is unclear...

Gene Simmons & His Band "On Tour"

March 2, 2017 - Drai's Nightclub, Vancouver, BC, Canada
**PRIVATE SHOW
Promoter: Drai's / YPO Edge
Other act(s): None.
Reported audience: ~300
Set list(s): Deuce / Radioactive / I Love It Loud / Christine Sixteen / Treat Her Right (Roy Head) / Cold Gin / Calling Dr. Love / Don't Let Go (En Vogue) / Money (Floyd) / Parasite / 634-5789 (Wilson Pickett) / **Unknown Song** / War Machine / Nothin' To Lose / Let Me Go, Rock 'N Roll / Rock and Roll All Nite
Notes:
- Held in conjunction with the Young Professionals Organization Edge, an international business leaders' convention that Gene had been attending at the Vancouver Convention Centre from March 1–3.
- Drai's was a then exclusive new 8,000-square-foot club, located inside the Vancouver Trump International Hotel & Tower that would officially open the following night.
- Gene was backed by a group which included Phil Shouse, Jeremy Asbrock, and Ryan Cook on guitars. The solo shows scratched multiple itches for Gene. Probably most importantly, the kept him busy. Many shows came with few demands from promoters other than putting on a great show and dig out some songs that would otherwise never be performed by KISS. He recalled, "I never did solo tours or performances in 44 years. KISS satisfied everything ... But when we're not playing, I like to keep busy ... By the way, this doesn't mean anything in terms of KISS. KISS continues to tour the world. We have a great time together. But the

band doesn't play anywhere near as much as I like to get out there. This is just an excuse for me to play hooky" (Windsor Star, 8/16/2017).

- Originally announced as the drummer for the project, Jarred Pope (drums) would ultimately be too busy with obligations with Damon Johnson and Kaato.

- The first 30 minutes of this show (through "Calling Dr. Love") was streamed live on Facebook. The rest of the set is as detailed by a band member's post of the actual set sheet.

March 18 - Agora Theatre, Cleveland, OH
Promoter: Wizard World Comic Con Presents
Other act(s): None.
Reported audience: (600 capacity)
Set list(s): Radioactive / Deuce / Nothin' to Lose / Jam (band intros) / Calling Dr. Love / Almost Human / Cold Gin / I Love It Loud / Got Love For Sale / Parasite / Plaster Caster / Charisma / See You Tonite / Christine Sixteen / Johnny B. Goode / War Machine / Let Me Go, Rock 'N' Roll / Rock and Roll All Nite
Notes:
- Gene's proper public solo debut with His Band for the then new venture, Wizard World Touring. By the time this show took place the band included drummer Paul Simmons. Opening with "Radioactive" was unusual, with the intro to the studio version generally being used instead.
- According to Gene, "Outside of KISS, I've never done a solo tour. I never did anything like that. Every once in a while, I'll jump up on stage and do a song with somebody. Johnny Depp and I did a few songs together, a few other knuckleheads, but that's about it... When Wizard World and I agreed to do five events together, the idea of jumping up onstage and gulping it on for an hour or so came up. And I got a great bunch of guys, real rocking guys who are gonna get up with me, and we'll play all the hits and have ourselves a good old time" (CantonRep.com, 3/2/2017).

- Gene honored Chuck Berry, who had passed away that day, with a rendition of "Johnny B. Goode" during his set. Gene recalled the importance of Chuck: "The backbone of rock 'n' roll is guitar... Without the electric guitar, you wouldn't have rock 'n' roll. Not in this form. There was Little Richard and Jerry Lee Lewis who did it on keyboards, but intrinsically, when the solo comes up, you want to hear some guy wail. Chuck Berry was the guy. He was the guy that Keith Richards and George Harrison learned from and, clearly, without Chuck Berry, there wouldn't have been a rock 'n' roll, or there certainly would have been a completely different form of it" (KMUW.org, 4/6/2017).
- The band was assembled via Ryan Cook, who had once been a member of Hair of the Dog and was managed by McGhee Entertainment. A member of The Big Rock Show, Ryan had also participated in the KISS Kruise.

April 6 - Southwind Casino, Braman, OK
Promoter: Wizard World Comic Con Presents
Other act(s): Drowning Pool, Taddy Porter, Nicnos, BC & The Big Rig, Jenny Wood
Reported audience: (5,000 capacity)
Set list(s): Deuce / Radioactive / Nothin' to Lose / Calling Dr. Love / Almost Human / Shout It Out Loud / Cold Gin / I Love It Loud / Got Love for Sale / Parasite / Plaster Caster / Charisma / Watchin' You / Domino / Christine Sixteen / Let Me Go, Rock 'N Roll / Rock and Roll All Nite
Notes:
- Part of the "Rock Fest 2017" outdoor festival. Gene and Paul had previously partnered with the Kaw Nation to bring one of their Rock & Brews franchises to the casino, having broken ground at the site in January.
- The Gene Simmons band's lineup in April included Jimmy Herman (Carrie Underwood) and Ryan Wariner (Gary Allan) filling in for Jeremy and Ryan on guitars — both had previously performed guest slots with Thee Rock 'N' Roll Residency.

- "ICT Rock Girl," 4th grader joined Gene on stage for "Shout It Out Loud," after being spotted playing in the parking lot.

April 8 - The Pageant, St. Louis, MO
Promoter: Wizard World Comic Con Presents
Other act(s): Amorath
Reported audience: (2,300 capacity)
Set list(s): Deuce / Radioactive / Nothin' to Lose / Calling Dr. Love / Almost Human / Cold Gin / Jam (band intros) / I Love It Loud / Got Love for Sale / Parasite / Plaster Caster / Charisma / Watchin' You / Domino / Christine Sixteen / Johnny B. Goode / Let Me Go, Rock 'N Roll / Rock and Roll All Nite
Notes:
- A contest was held via KSHE-95 to find an opening band for the show. According to Gene, "Nowadays, to be a new band is the hardest thing in the world. You have to give music away for free. You can't earn a living. I wanted to reach out to new bands and give them a shot" (St. Louis Post-Dispatch, 3/31/2017).
- The following day Gene attended Chuck Berry's funeral where he delivered what was described as an unplanned, but touching, eulogy. Gene was particularly disappointed at the lack of rock 'n' roll notables from Chuck's funeral.
- An excellent AUD recording circulates from this show.

June 2 - Trocadero Theater, Philadelphia, PA
Promoter: Wizard World Comic Con Presents
Other act(s): Creem Circus
Reported audience: (1,200 capacity)
Set list(s): Deuce / Shout It Out Loud / Nothin' to Lose / Calling Dr. Love / Do You Love Me? / I Love It Loud / Parasite / Radioactive / Christine Sixteen / Sweet & Dirty Love / Got Love for Sale / Cold Gin / Charisma / Domino / Boom Boom (Band Intros Jam) / Rice Pudding (Jeff Beck) / Let Me Go, Rock 'N' Roll / Rock and Roll All Nite
Notes:

- Gene had flown in from London on June 1, KISS having then just completed a run of European concert dates throughout May.
- A young fan joined the band on guitar for "Parasite." Guitarists Ryan Cook and Jeremy Asbrock returned to the band's lineup.

June 9 - Hoosier Park Racing & Casino, Anderson (Indianapolis), IN

Promoter: Hoosier Park Sounds of Summer / Live Nation
Other act(s): None.
Reported audience: (4,500 capacity)
Set list(s): Deuce / Shout It Out Loud / Nothin' to Lose / Calling Dr. Love / Radioactive / I Love It Loud / Do You Love Me? / Got Love for Sale / Sweet & Dirty Love / Parasite / Cold Gin / Rice Pudding (Jeff Beck) / Charisma / Domino / Christine Sixteen / Let Me Go, Rock 'N' Roll / Rock and Roll All Nite

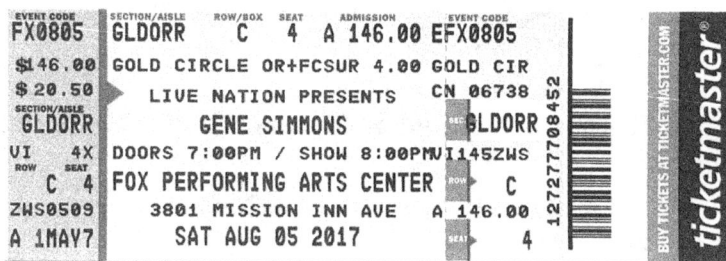

August 4 - Harrah's Resort Events Center, Valley Center, CA **CANCELLED
August 5 - Fox Performing Arts Center, Riverside, CA **CANCELLED

Notes:
- Announced in June, both dates were cancelled in late July. While no official explanation was given, soft ticket sales seem to have been the reason. Also occurring around the same time was a change in drummers for the band, with Paul Simmons being replaced by Brent Fitz.

August 11 - Shooting Star Casino, Mahnomen, MN
Promoter: Shooting Star Casino
Other act(s): None.
Reported audience: (1,750 capacity)
Set list(s): Deuce / Shout It Out Loud / I Love It loud / Cold Gin / Got Love for Sale / Do You Love Me? / Boom Boom (band intros) / Wall of Sound / Charisma / Watchin' You / She / Parasite / Nothin' to Lose / Calling Dr. Love / Christine Sixteen / Rock and Roll All Nite / When You Wish upon a Star

August 12 - North Star Mohican Casino & Resort, Bowler, WI
Promoter: North Star Mohican Casino
Other act(s): None.
Reported audience: (1,000 capacity)
Set list(s): Deuce / Shout It Out Loud / I Love It loud / Calling Dr. Love / Do You Love Me? / Radioactive / Parasite / Cold Gin / Got Love for Sale / Boom Boom (band intros) / Wall of Sound / Charisma / Christine Sixteen / Plaster Caster / Let Me Go, Rock 'N' Roll / Rock and Roll All Nite

August 25 - The Colosseum at Caesars Windsor, Windsor, ON, Canada
Promoter: C3 Presents / Caesars Entertainment
Other act(s): None.
Reported audience: 3,661 / 4,934 (74.2%)
Reported gross: $182,220
Set list(s): Deuce / Shout It Out Loud / I Love It loud / Christine Sixteen / You're Going to Lose That Girl / Got Love for Sale / Do You Love Me? / Radioactive / Wall of Sound / Charisma / Jam / Watchin' You / She / Plaster Caster / Parasite / Calling Dr. Love / Cold Gin / Rock and Roll All Nite
Notes:
- Raj Mangipudi, who portrays "The Demon" in Michigan KISS tribute band Detroit Rock City, sang "Parasite" with the band.

- From a local review: "Windsor became party central on Friday night as KISS founder Gene Simmons rolled into The Colosseum with a solo band for a special birthday bash that drew fans from as far away as Toronto and the outer reaches of Michigan to celebrate the bass player's 68th birthday. Gene brought the energy and excitement of an intimate KISS Kruise performance to the massive casino stage and the majority of the 5,000 in attendance loved it. The set was filled with KISS classics, songs that haven't been played in years and several rarities, including a few nuggets never performed live until this tour. Not wearing the outrageous face paint and demon costume he's known for, Simmons was relaxed and casual for the 90-plus minute performance and he graciously thanked his family, fans and band members for multiple outbursts of Happy Birthday, including a moment where his wife Shannon Tweed-Simmons and daughter Sophie Simmons rolled out a giant birthday cake. With Shannon and Sophie in tow, it felt like a family event, giving the show an extremely intimate feel" (YQG Rocks, 8/28/2017).

August 26 - The Park West, Chicago, IL
Promoter: Live Nation
Other act(s):
Reported audience: (900 capacity)
Set list(s): Deuce / Shout It Out Loud / I Love It loud / Calling Dr. Love / You're Going to Lose That Girl / Ladies Room / Got Love for Sale / Do You Love Me? / Radioactive / Wall of Sound / Charisma / Watchin' You / She / Parasite / Cold Gin / Rock and Roll All Nite
Notes:
- Conducted in conjunction with the Wizard World Comic Con, "Plaster Caster" was included on the set list (after "Parasite) but was not performed.

September 8 - American Music Theater, Lancaster, PA
Promoter: in-house

Other act(s): Creem Circus
Reported audience: (1,600 capacity)
Set list(s): Deuce / Shout It Out Loud / I Love It loud / You're Going to Lose That Girl / Ladies Room / Got Love for Sale / Do You Love Me? / Radioactive / Ladies in Waiting / Wall of Sound / Charisma / Watchin' You / She / Parasite / Plaster Caster / Cold Gin / Rock and Roll All Nite
Notes:
- A Millersville University student joined Gene to perform "Parasite."

September 16 - Loretta Lynn's Ranch, Hurricane Mills, TN **CANCELLED

Promoter: Mike Axle
Other act(s): Skid Row, Slaughter, The Big Rock Show
Notes:
- Announced in Dec. 2016, part of a 10-day event running Sep. 14–24, the Bike Week Nashville event ran into challenges when the original venue withdrew due to a contractual dispute. The promoter was also ordered to cease selling tickets for the event, which should not have been placed on sale without the event having applied for or been granted at mass gathering license by the Tennessee Department of Health. By early January, the date had been removed from Gene's touring schedule. Ultimately, authorities were left searching for the promoter, who had a lengthy criminal history and previous convictions for fraud and theft.

September 20 - CHS Field, Minneapolis, MN

Promoter: The Children Matter
Other act(s): Cheap Trick, Don Felder, The Jayhawks, Flipp
Reported audience: ~3,000
Set list(s): Deuce / Shout It Out Loud / Nothin' to Lose / Do You Love Me? / Charisma / Radioactive / Christine Sixteen / Calling Dr. Love / Parasite (with Ace) / Cold Gin (with Ace) / Shock Me (with Ace) / Rock and Roll All Nite (with Ace)

Notes:
- From a local review: "Original KISS members Gene Simmons and Ace Frehley reunited for the event, their first joint appearance in public since the group was inducted into the Rock and Roll Hall of Fame in 2014. Unlike that terse ceremony, however, this time they came to play — their first performance together in 16 years. They didn't rock 'n' roll all night; curfew was 10:15pm. But the KISS cronies did get to party all day with a couple of fellow Hall of Fame acts also on the lineup: '70s hit-makers Cheap Trick and form Eagles guitarist Don Felder... Simmons' willingness to yield the spotlight to Frehley underlined his commitment to the cause. He helped organize the concert on behalf of a Twin Cities-based charity he has worked with before... The charity's overall focus is feeding and aiding children worldwide, but after Hurricane Harvey hit in late August, the concert's theme turned specifically to assistance in Houston and surrounding areas" (Minneapolis Star Tribune, 9/21/2017).
- Matter.ngo benefit concert that raises over $1 million for hurricane relief.
- Ace Frehley joined Gene onstage to perform several songs.

September 23 - Hall D @ Edmonton Expo Centre, Edmonton, AB, Canada

Promoter: Live Nation/Edmonton Expo
Other act(s): Savage Playground
Reported audience: ~500 / 4,000 (12.50%)
Set list: Deuce / Shout It Out Loud / I Love It Loud / Do You Love Me? / Charisma / Radioactive / Christine Sixteen / Calling Dr. Love / Boom, Boom (band intros) / Plaster Caster / Domino / She / Ladies in Waiting / Rock and Roll All Nite
Notes:
- Small show with venue clearly not expected to utilize anywhere near its capacity.
- Gene essentially played less than an hour during a set hindered by tuning issues. Sound was brutal, and the crowd

was small. However, even with the shortened duration, no songs were cut from the planned set.

- An excellent AUD recording circulates from this show.

October 15 - Super Arena, Saitama, Japan
Promoter: Creative Man Productions, Ltd.
Other act(s): Michael Schenker Fest (HL), Meshuggah, Black Star Riders, Loudness, Outrage, Cry Venom (opener)
Reported audience: (22,500 capacity)
Set list(s): Deuce / Parasite / I Love It Loud / Cold Gin / Boom, Boom (band intros) / Do You Love Me? / Shout It Out Loud / Calling Dr. Love / War Machine / Wall of Sound / Got Love for Sale / Watchin' You / She / Let Me Go, Rock 'N' Roll / Rock and Roll All Nite
Notes:
- Loud Park 2017 festival with the band playing the "Big Rock" stage.

October 17 - Namba Hatch, Osaka, Japan
Promoter: Creative Man Productions, Ltd.
Other act(s): None.
Reported audience: (2,513 capacity)

Set list(s): Deuce / Parasite / I Love It Loud / Cold Gin / Boom, Boom (band intros) / Radioactive / You're Going to Lose That Girl / Do You Love Me? / Domino / Shout It Out Loud / Calling Dr. Love / Christine Sixteen / War Machine / Watchin' You / Wall of Sound / Let Me Go, Rock 'N' Roll / Rock and Roll All Nite

Notes:

- A mass-market bootleg CD is available from this show.

October 21 - Teatro al Aire Libre, La Paz, Bolivia

Promoter: La Biblia Del Metal Producciones

Other act(s): Dee Snider, Tarja Turunen, Malon, Tierra Santa, Alma Eterna, Maldita Suerte

Reported audience: (9,000 capacity)

Set list(s): Deuce / Parasite / I Love It Loud / Shout It Out Loud / Calling Dr. Love / Nothin' to Lose / Do You Love Me? / Domino / Charisma / War Machine / Goin' Blind / Watchin' You / Cold Gin / Rock and Roll All Nite

Notes:

- Part of the "Screamin' Festival".

October 24 - Groove, Buenos Aires, Argentina

Promoter: Rock y Reggae Producciones

Other act(s): El Buen Salvaje

Reported audience: (1,700 capacity)

Set list(s): Deuce / Nothin' to Lose / Parasite / Shout It Out Loud / Boom, Boom (band intros) / Do You Love Me? / I Love It Loud / War Machine / Goin' Blind / Calling Dr. Love / Plaster Caster / Domino / Charisma / Watchin' You / Rock and Roll All Nite

Notes:

- Originally scheduled for the Estadio Cubierto Malvinas Argentinas.

October 26 - Teatro Cariola, Santiago, Chile

Promoter: Transistor

Other act(s): None.

Reported audience: (1,270 capacity)
Set list(s): Deuce / Nothin' to Lose / Shout It Out Loud /
Parasite / Boom, Boom (band intros) / Do You Love Me? / I
Love It Loud / War Machine / Goin' Blind / Plaster Caster /
Calling Dr. Love / Radioactive / Domino / Charisma /
Watchin' You / Rock and Roll All Nite
Notes:
- Even with 2:1 tickets and discounted sales, this show was
lightly attended, competing with other concerts at the same
venue that week including In Flames and Sepultura.
- Fantastic video of the full show circulates.

October 28 - Parque Fundidora, Monterrey, Mexico
Promoter: OCESA / CIE
Other act(s): Incubus, Deftones, In Flames, Kreator, Tarja
Turunen, Exodus, Baroness, Frank Carter & The
Rattlesnakes, RavenEye,
Reported audience: 5,054 / 6,844 (73.85%)
Reported gross: $250,925
Set list(s): Deuce / Parasite / War Machine / I Love It Loud /
Nothin' to Lose / Shout It Out Loud / Charisma / Domino /
Watchin' You / Let Me Go, Rock 'N' Roll / Rock and Roll All
Nite
Notes:
- The "Corona Northside" festival. The GSB performed in
daylight, though the sun soon started disappearing
providing an interesting atmosphere... Shortened set due to
the festival format.

October 30 - Pepsi Center WTC, Mexico City, Mexico
Promoter: OCESA / CIE
Other act(s): None.
Reported audience: 3,050 / 4,838 (63.04%)
Reported gross: $55,741
Set list(s): Deuce / Nothin' to Lose / Shout It Out Loud /
Parasite / Boom, Boom (band intros) / Do You Love Me? / I
Love It Loud / Let Me Go, Rock 'N' Roll / War Machine /

Charisma / Domino / Goin' Blind / Watchin' You / La Bamba / Rock and Roll All Nite
Notes:
- Fantastic video of the full show circulates on YouTube. The show ended with boos and whistles from the fans when the band failed to return to the stage following "Rock and Roll All Nite."

November 1 - The Lynn Memorial Auditorium, Lynn, MA **POSTPONED
Notes:
- This show was postponed until Feb. 16, 2018.

November 12 - The VETS Auditorium, Providence, RI
Promoter: in-house / Professional Facilities Mgmt.
Other act(s): None.
Reported audience: 368 / 1,933 (19.04%)
Reported gross: $40,648
Set list(s): Deuce / Shout It Out Loud / Parasite / I Love It Loud / She / Calling Dr. Love / Christine Sixteen / Let Me Go, Rock 'N' Roll / War Machine / Goin' Blind / Charisma / Radioactive / Domino / Rock and Roll All Nite
Notes:
- Gene received the key to the city from a local city councilor during the show, which was conducted in conjunction with the RI Comic Con.
- A heckler disrupting the show caused a delay while he's ejected. The heckler was reportedly the now deceased Anal C**t guitarist Josh Martin, who became frustrated with the extended mid-concert break and yelled, "Is this a fucking joke?", "Shut up and play your guitar!" and "Play some music, PLEASE!"

November 18 - Convention Center, Austin, TX **CANCELLED
Promoter: Wizard World Comic Con Presents
Notes:

- Gene's participation at this final scheduled Wizard World event was cancelled due to a "scheduling conflict." Originally part of the schedule of 5 shows announced in January 2017.

January 23, 2018 - Mercy Lounge, Nashville, TN **GUEST APPEARANCE
Notes:
- Gene made a guest appearance with his band mates at their Thee Rock 'N' Roll Residency show, joining them for "Deuce" and "Shout It Out Loud."

February 1 - Adelaide Entertainment Centre, Hindmarsh (Adelaide), SA, Australia **POSTPONED
February 2 - Enmore Theatre, Newtown (Sydney), NSW, Australia **POSTPONED
February 3 - Margaret Court Arena, Melbourne, VIC, Australia **POSTPONED
February 6 - The Tivoli, Fortitude Valley, QLD, Australia **POSTPONED
Notes:
- These dates were postponed until later in the year on Jan. 16 due to the Australian Vault experience dates being moved to later in the year.

February 16 - The Lynn Memorial Auditorium, Lynn, MA
Promoter: Lynn Auditorium Presents
Other act(s): Watts
Reported audience: (2,112 capacity)
Set list(s): Deuce / Shout It Out Loud / Are You Ready / Parasite / Calling Dr. Love / Do You Love Me? / Almost Human / Long Tall Sally / I / Help! / I Love It Loud / War Machine / Strutter / Sweet Pain / She's So European / Charisma / It's My Life / Rock and Roll All Nite
Notes:
- A blind fan, Brian, joined the band to sing "Calling Dr. Love." Gene later posted, He "proceeded to tear the roof

off the concert hall, steal the show and upstage the entire band. See for yourself, what this remarkable young man did. When I grow up, I want to be just like him" (KISS Online). Extreme's Gary Cherone joined the band to sing "Strutter."

- From a local review: "Friday evening at Lynn Auditorium, Gene Simmons and his band rocked and rolled all night. Well, technically, it was only 90 minutes. But it was an insanely entertaining, freewheeling 90 minutes that contained many surprises, special guests and thrilled fans of all ages. Simmons, bassist/vocalist for Rock and Roll Hall of Famers KISS, had postponed this show from Nov. 1. The wait was worth it. His 18-song set was comprised almost entirely of KISS songs, many of them true obscurities, including a couple that he claimed had never been performed live. This wasn't KISS — Simmons, in jeans and black shirt, wasn't wearing his Demon makeup and there was no spitting of fire and fake blood — but it was still a heck of a lot of fun. A few fans arrived with their faces made up, including a young boy, dubbed Little Gene Simmons, who made it onto the stage with about 30 other kids during the set-closing 'Rock and Roll All Nite'... Simmons was an affable host, contradicting his reputation as a jerk, and insisted that the black mop covering his head is his real hair, drawing laughs and disbelieving head-shakes from the crowd. To my eyes, it looked like the worst, cheapest wig available. Oddly, there was no merch table in the lobby" (Lynn Daily Item, 2/17/2018).

- Audience filmed video circulates from this show.

May 2 - Surf Ballroom & Museum, Clear Lake, IA

Promoter: in-house
Other act(s): Bad Authority
Reported audience: (2,100 capacity)
Set list(s): Deuce / Shout It Out Loud / Are You Ready / It's My Life / Calling Dr. Love / I Love It Loud / Love Theme from KISS / Long Tall Sally / War Machine / Fits Like A Glove /

Strutter / Sweet Pain / She's So European / World Without Heroes / I / Charisma / Let Me Go, Rock 'N' Roll / Rock and Roll All Nite
Notes:
- During the show Gene was awarded honorary lifetime membership to the 1st Iowa Infantry Association. This venue is famed as being the location of the final performances of Buddy Holly, Ritchie Valens and J.P. "The Big Bopper" Richardson, prior to their fateful flight in the early morning of Feb. 3, 1959.

May 3 - Arcada Theatre, Saint Charles, IL
Promoter: in-house / Onesti Entertainment
Other act(s): Teeze
Reported audience: (897 capacity)
Set list(s): Deuce / Shout It Out Loud / Are You Ready / It's My Life / Calling Dr. Love / I Love It Loud / Love Theme from KISS / Long Tall Sally / War Machine / Fits Like A Glove / Sweet Pain / Do You Love Me? / World Without Heroes / I / Charisma / Let Me Go, Rock 'N' Roll / Rock and Roll All Nite
Notes:
- Gene ended the evening having to shout at one fan, who'd come on stage for the final song who kept bumping into him during the song.

May 4 - Foellinger Theatre, Fort Wayne, IN
Promoter: Pacific Coast Concerts / in-house
Other act(s): None
Reported audience: (2,751 capacity)
Set list(s): Deuce / Shout It Out Loud / Are You Ready / It's My Life / Christine Sixteen / I Love It Loud / Love Theme from KISS / Long Tall Sally / Fits Like A Glove / Sweet Pain / Do You Love Me? / World Without Heroes / I / Charisma / Let Me Go, Rock 'N' Roll / Rock and Roll All Nite
Notes:
- This engagement netted the Fort Wayne Parks & Recreation Department $8,648.

June 2 - Stora scenen @ Gröna Lund, Stockholm, Sweden
Promoter: in-house
Other act(s): None
Reported audience: (22,000 capacity)
Set list(s): Deuce / Shout It Out Loud / Parasite / I Love It Loud / Unholy (partial) / Love Theme from KISS / War Machine / She's So European / Calling Dr. Love / Charisma / I / Cold Gin / Do You Love Me? / It's My Life / Are You Ready / Watchin' You / Fits Like A Glove / Let Me Go, Rock 'N' Roll / Rock and Roll All Nite / Christine Sixteen
Notes:
- A 15-year-old kid held up a sign begging to play drums and Gene obliged him. He came back onstage at the end of the show for an impromptu rendition of "Christine Sixteen."
- A fantastic multi-cam BluRay circulates from this show.

July 15 - R. Jelínek Distillery, Vizovice, Czech Republic
Promoter: Pragokoncert Bohemia, a.s.
Other act(s): Korpiklaani, Doro, Orden Ogan, Destuction, Masterplan, Silent Stream of Godless, Alkehol, Nervosa, Salamandra
Reported audience: ~unknown.
Set list(s): Deuce / Parasite / Shout It Out Loud / Are You Ready / I Love It Loud / Long Tall Sally / Love Theme from KISS / War Machine / Almost Human / Do You Love Me? / I / Calling Dr. Love / Let Me Go, Rock 'N' Roll / Rock and Roll All Nite
Notes:
- The bands performed on the "Rock Face" stage for this "Masters of Rock" festival appearance. Doro joined the band for "War Machine."

July 16 - Gasometer B Halle, Vienna, Austria
Promoter: Mind over Matter
Other act(s): The Weight
Reported audience: (4,200 capacity)

Set list(s): Deuce / Shout It Out Loud / Parasite / Are You Ready / Let Me Go, Rock 'N' Roll / Charisma / Long Tall Sally / Do You Love Me? / I / Almost Human / I Love It Loud / Love Theme from KISS / War Machine / Calling Dr. Love / Cold Gin / Rock and Roll All Nite

Notes:

- From a local review: "Accompanied by three standard-looking guitarists who not only know how to swing their implements, but also what Gene Simmons' partner in KISS, Paul Stanley, unfortunately cannot do: sound like Paul Stanley... The concert sounds paradoxically better than KISS and at the same time fader, because the makeup, costumes, and the big show, so the hint of the something special, was missing. Second downside: Inexplicably, Simmons, who has solo material for ten concerts, brought only one solo number ('Are You Ready?'). The rest was KISS stuff, with the exception of a wonderfully swinging 'Long Tall Sally' and a rock 'n' roll-jam that sounds more like a rehearsal-room-joke. After all, Simmons allows himself to unpack a few rarities, such as 'Charisma' from the 'Dynasty' album, 'I' from the totally undervalued 'The Elder' and 'Almost Human' from 'Love Gun'... Conclusion: great fun for diehard fans" (Translation from of kurier.at, 8/28/2018).

July 18 - Rockhal, Esch-sur-Alzette, Luxembourg
Promoter: in-house
Other act(s): The Michael Shepherd Band
Reported audience: (6,500 capacity)
Set list(s): Deuce / Shout It Out Loud / Are You Ready / Nothin' to Lose / Parasite / Let Me Go, Rock 'N' Roll / Do You Love Me? / All the Way / Charisma / Long Tall Sally / I Love It Loud / War Machine / I / Calling Dr. Love / Rock and Roll All Nite

July 19 - Poppodium 013, Tilburg, Netherlands
Promoter: in-house
Other act(s): The Blackmordia

Reported audience: (3,000 capacity)

Set list(s): Deuce / Shout It Out Loud / Are You Ready / Radioactive / Parasite / She's So European / La Bamba / Let Me Go, Rock 'N' Roll / I Was Made for Lovin' You / Do You Love Me? / All the Way / Charisma / Long Tall Sally / I Love It Loud / I / Domino (partial) / War Machine / Calling Dr. Love / Rock and Roll All Nite

Notes:

- A fan joins the band to perform "Parasite."
- A stunning fan authored multi-cam BluRay circulates from this show.

July 20 - Turbinenhalle, Oberhausen, Germany

Promoter: MBM Live

Other act(s): Thunder, The Brew, Reds'Cool

Reported audience: (4,000 capacity)

Set list(s): Deuce / Are You Ready / Shout It Out Loud / Parasite / She's So European / Unholy / Do You Love Me? /

I Was Made for Lovin' You / Long Tall Sally / Let Me Go, Rock 'N' Roll / Watchin' You / Love Theme from KISS / War Machine / I / Charisma / Radioactive / I Love It Loud / Domino / Ladies Room / Almost Human / Goin' Blind / Calling Dr. Love / Rock and Roll All Nite

Notes:

- "Rocks" magazine 10th anniversary celebration show.

August 10 - James Donaldson Park, Grand Forks, BC, Canada

Promoter: CannaFest

Other act(s): Burton Cummings (HL), Mark Farner's American Band, Dr. Fun & the Nightout, The Tokanees, Mad Dog 20/20

Reported audience: (10,000 capacity)

Set list(s): Deuce / Shout It Out Loud / Are You Ready / Calling Dr. Love / Parasite / Do You Love Me? / I Was Made for Lovin' You / Long Tall Sally / Let Me Go, Rock 'N' Roll / Love Theme from KISS / War Machine / All the Way / I / Charisma / Radioactive / I Love It Loud / Rock and Roll All Nite

Notes:

- Event held at the CannaFest Festival grounds. Darby Mills, who had been lead singer for the Headpins when they opened for KISS in 1983, sang "I Was Made for Lovin' You" wearing Gene's warpaint. A young teen joined the band as guest drummer on "Calling Dr. Love."

August 25 - Acceleration de Camion St-Joseph, Saint-Joseph-de-Beauce, QC, Canada

Promoter: Benoit Gagné

Other act(s): James Barker Band

Reported audience: (55,000 capacity)

Set list(s): Deuce / Shout It Out Loud / Are You Ready / Calling Dr. Love / Radioactive / Charisma / Do You Love Me? / Plaster Caster / Long Tall Sally / Sweet Pain / Love Theme from KISS / War Machine / I Love It Loud / She's So

European / She / Jam / Let Me Go, Rock 'N' Roll / Rock and Roll All Nite
Notes:
- This show was in conjunction with a tractor-pull event.
- Partial video from the event has been posted on YouTube.

August 28 - Adelaide Entertainment Centre Theatre, Hindmarsh (Adelaide), SA, Australia
Promoter: TEG Live
Other act(s): Ace Frehley
Reported audience: ~1,400 / 1,950 (71.80%)
Ace Frehley set list: Parasite / Hard Times / 2,000 Man / Rock Soldiers / Rip It Out / Love Gun (Phil vocals) / Rocket Ride / Strange Ways (Chris vocals) / Talk to Me / New York Groove / Shock Me / Cold Gin
Gene Simmons set list: Deuce / Shout It Out Loud / Nothin' to Lose / Calling Dr. Love / Radioactive / Charisma / I Was Made for Lovin' You / Do You Love Me? / Plaster Caster / Sweet Pain / Love Theme from KISS / War Machine / She's So European / I Love It Loud / All the Way / Let Me Go, Rock 'N' Roll / Rock and Roll All Nite
Notes:
- From tour PR: " In his first solo tour of Australia, fans can look forward to Gene blasting through his classics — 'Charisma,' 'Radioactive,' 'Mr. Make Believe' — plus tracks

from the first KISS album right up to now. This will include material from LPs such as 'Dynasty,' 'Unmasked' and 'The Elder' which were hits specifically in Australia. Gene will perform songs that have never been played live by KISS and many of which have never been performed live in Australia before, along with songs from his solo album" (TEG).

- A female audience member, Rose, sang "I Was Made for Lovin' You" with Gene. Ace joined KISS for the final song of the night.

August 30 - Festival Hall, West Melbourne, VIC, Australia
Promoter: TEG Live
Other act(s): Ace Frehley
Reported audience: ~1,100 / 5,000 (22.00%)

Ace Frehley set list: Parasite / Hard Times / 2,000 Man / Rock Soldiers / Rip It Out / Love Gun (Phil vocals) / Rocket Ride / Strange Ways / New York Groove / Shock Me / Detroit Rock City / Cold Gin

Gene Simmons set list: Deuce / Shout It Out Loud / Are You Ready / Calling Dr. Love / Radioactive / I / Almost Human / Charisma / I Was Made for Lovin' You / Do You Love Me? / Long Tall Sally / Plaster Caster / Sweet Pain / Love Theme from KISS / War Machine / I Love It Loud / She's So European / Let Me Go, Rock 'N' Roll / Rock and Roll All Nite

- A guitarist from the audience joined the band for "Calling Dr. Love" while Amy Lehpamer sang "I Was Made for Lovin' You."

- Ace joined Gene for the final two songs and goofed around with a bit of "Torpedo Girl."

- An AUD recording circulates from this show.

August 31 - Enmore Theatre, Newtown (Sydney), NSW, Australia

Promoter: TEG Live
Other act(s): Ace Frehley
Reported audience: (1,600 capacity)
Ace Frehley set list: Same as Aug. 30
Gene Simmons set list: Shout it Out Loud / I / Are You Ready / War Machine / Long Tall Sally / Calling Dr. Love / Charisma / She's So European / Love Theme from KISS / Let Me Go, Rock 'N' Roll / I Was Made for Lovin' You / Do You Love Me? / Watchin' You / Radioactive / I Love It Loud / Plaster Caster / Deuce / Rock and Roll All Nite

Notes:
- Virginia Lillye sang "I Was Made for Lovin' You" while Ace joined Gene for the final two songs.

- A fan placed a photo of Vinnie Vincent on the stage with the note, "Gene, please call me xxxox."

- An AUD recording circulates from this show.

September 1 - The Tivoli, Fortitude Valley (Brisbane), QLD, Australia
Promoter: TEG Live
Other act(s): Ace Frehley
Reported audience: (1,500 capacity)
Ace Frehley set list: Same as Aug. 30
Gene Simmons set list: Shout it Out Loud / I / Are You Ready / War Machine / Calling Dr. Love / Charisma / She's So European / Love Theme from KISS / Let Me Go, Rock 'N' Roll / Radioactive / I Was Made for Lovin' You / Do You Love Me? / Long Tall Sally / Watchin' You / I Love It Loud / Plaster Caster / Deuce / Rock and Roll All Nite
Notes:
- An audience member sings "I Was Made for Lovin' You" and Ace joined Gene for the final two songs.
- From a local review: "It wasn't quite a fully-fledged KISS reunion, but it was probably the closest fans are going to get. Band co-founder Gene Simmons and original guitarist Ace Frehley last night shared a Queensland stage for the first time since the so-called KISS Farewell Tour 17 1/2 years ago. It was ostensibly a Simmons solo tour, but Frehley the 'Spaceman' has been sharing the limelight as opening act, before joining 'The Demon' on-stage at the show's climax. Both played KISS classics and tunes from their solo catalogues at the Tivoli show. Earlier in the day the pair had pressed the flesh with a few dozen über-fans who each had shelled out $US2000 for Simmons' The Vault — literally a safe full of rare recordings and other paraphernalia. Simmons played the opening track from The Vault, 'Are You Ready,' at last night's show. For his KISS numbers, he relied on members of his backing band to substitute in for KISS frontman Paul Stanley's vocals" (Brisbane Courier-Mail, 9/2/2018).
- Following the brief tour, Gene returned home, and Ace headed for Japan for dates in Tokyo and Osaka.

**September 8 - River Spirit Event Center, Tulsa, OK
CANCELLED
Promoter: in-house
Notes:
- This show was cancelled July 18 due to a "scheduling conflict" — such as Gene's band being in Japan backing Ace Frehley!

September 15 - Wolf Den @ Mohegan Sun Casino & Resort, Uncasville, CT **POSTPONED
Promoter: in-house
Notes:
- This show was postponed on July 23 due to a "scheduling conflict." Dates around this period were replaced with 7-Eleven in-store appearances to promote Gene's Moneybag soda partnership, along with Gene's participation in the Toronto Money Show on Sept. 14.

September 21 - Turning Stone Resort Casino Event Center, Verona, NY
Promoter: in-house
Other act(s): None.
Reported audience: 649 / 1,204 (53.90%)
Reported gross: $43,674
Set list: Deuce / Shout it Out Loud / Calling Dr. Love / Charisma / Are You Ready / Do You Love Me? / I / Plaster Caster / Long Tall Sally / Sweet Pain / I Love It Loud / Love Theme from KISS / War Machine / She's So European / Let Me Go, Rock 'N' Roll / Rock and Roll All Nite
Notes:
- Earlier in the day, an in-store appearance at a 7-Eleven store in Syracuse, to promote the Moneybag soda line, was also scheduled. Other events were scheduled in Rochester (18th) and other Upstate New York locations... Gene also took a break during the show to conduct a live commercial to promote his Moneybags soda. He threw baked goods into the audience too...

- A fan removed her bra for Gene to use as his sweat cloth for the rest of the show...
- Likely to be the last Gene Simmons Band show for some time with KISS' "End of the Road" Tour scheduled for 2019. However, Ace Frehley would opt to replace his band with members of Gene's band plus drummer Matt Starr, at least for the KISS Kruise VIII...
- An AUD recording circulates from this show.

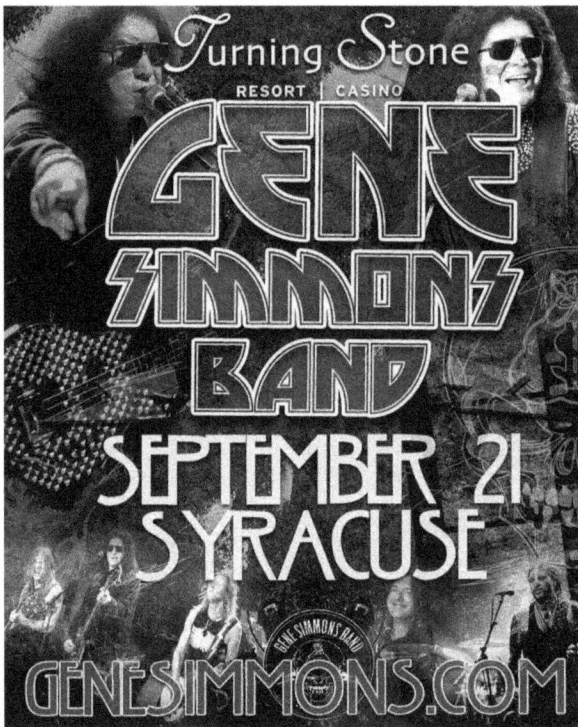

www.ingramcontent.com/pod-product-compliance
Lightning Source LLC
Chambersburg PA
CBHW031556040426
42452CB00006B/327